10 Commandments
Of A Successful Marriage

Published by:
Gita Publishing House
Sadhu Vaswani Mission,
10, Sadhu Vaswani Path,
Pune 411 001, (India).
gph@sadhuvaswani.org
www.dadavaswanisbooks.org

Fifth Edition

ISBN: 978-93-80743-32-5

Printed by:
Mehta Offset Pvt. Ltd.
Mehta House,
A-16, Naraina Industrial Area II,
New Delhi 110 028, (India).
Phone : +91-11-45670222
info@mehtaoffset.com

10 Commandments
Of A Successful Marriage

J.P. VASWANI

Compiled by:

Dr. (Mrs.) Prabha Sampath
and
Krishna Kumari

Gita Publishing House
Pune, (India).
www.dadavaswanisbooks.org

Other Books By Dada J.P. Vaswani

Contents

Introduction

The Hindu scriptures refer to the married state as *Grihasta Ashrama*. May I draw your attention to the use of the word *ashrama* here; the *ashrama* is a place or a state that denotes discipline and restraint. Thus, marriage according to the Hindu ideals is not a pleasure hunting ground. It is not a license to do as one pleases. It is at once a discipline and a responsibility. In marriage, two persons – a man and a woman – offer the whole of their self, mind, body, and feelings to each other. They cease to live for their selfish ends; they live for each other, for their families and for the promotion and propagation of *dharma* or righteousness.

Hindu *shastras* emphasise the value of *grihasta ashrama* as fundamental to the well-being of society. This is because the people in the other three *ashramas* depend on the *grihasta* (householder) for sustenance and support. They need the *grihasta's* help to carry out their duties. As for the *grihasta*, he is permitted to earn his living by the right means in order to support his family, raise his children and perform those acts of charity and compassion that assist others in the three *ashramas*.

I often tell my married friends that they are lucky to be in the *grihasta ashrama*, where all they have to do is perform their duty well, in order to attain salvation. However, this is not as easy as it sounds! Saints and sages refer to the life of the *grihasta* as *jivayagna* – a life-long saga of service and sacrifice for family and society.

A Hindu marriage is also referred to as *kanyadaan* – a beautiful, but much misunderstood term.

There are very many *daans* or *dhanas* advocated by the Hindu scriptures. Of these, *kanyadaan* – the gift of a virgin girl – is stated to be the supreme *daan*. It is said that he who is blessed with the opportunity of bestowing this supreme *daan* in his lifetime, and he who is bestowed with this gift, are truly beloved of the Lord. The bride's parents 'give her away' to the groom, entrusting her to his loving care. Significant are the words that accompany this wonderful gesture: "I have nurtured this child upto this age, and am now handing her over to you for the progeny and prosperity of your family. Consider her as your own and be her guide and philosopher till she lives with you."

On the bridegroom's side, marriage is termed as *Pani-grahan* (acceptance of the hand). By this beautiful and significant gesture, the groom's family welcomes the bride into their home, and the groom enters the holy state of matrimony with her. He accepts her as his partner for life, vowing to protect her and look after her, invoking God's grace to help them both follow the path of virtue.

Another Sanskrit term for marriage is *vivaha*, which literally means "what supports or carries". The *vivaha* ceremony thus creates a union which supports and sustains a man and woman throughout their married life in the pursuit of *dharma* (righteousness.)

Of the sixteen *samskaras* (sacraments) associated with Hinduism, *vivaha* or marriage is considered to be the most sacred, for the *grihasta ashrama* is considered to be the basis of all the other *ashramas*. Therefore, Hindu scriptures eulogize *vivaha* in glowing terms.

Marriage is not meant to satisfy carnal desires. Rather, it is meant to assist one's spiritual progress, leading to God-realisation through a disciplined life. In marriage, a young man and woman practise selfdiscipline and self-control, even as they find support and companionship with the spouse and other members of the family, and learn to offer selfless service to society.

Marriage may be said to be a co-operative venture between husband and wife in the field of the four *purusharthas* – *dharma*, *artha*, *kama,* and *moksha*. It is the union of two souls, and this sacred union is formalised through sacrament.

Vivaha is also literally translated to mean upliftment. Marriage helps young couples to raise themselves towards God. The bond of marriage unites two souls so firmly that though they are physically two separate entities, their souls are merged into one harmonious whole. Together, they vow always to:

- Have faith in the Divine.

- Show love, devotion and compassion to one another.

- Help in each other's good deeds.

- Strive to keep their minds pure and virtuous.

- Be strong and righteous.

- Show respect and affection to each other's parents and families.

- Raise their children to be strong in body and mind and pure in spirit.

- Welcome guests to their home.

It is significant that in one of the rituals that form part of the Hindu marriage called *laja homa* (prayer for shared prosperity), husband and wife take turns to lead one another around the fire, signifying that both are capable of leadership and guidance.

The *saptapati* or seven steps which form part of the Hindu marriage ceremony symbolise the couple's commitment:

- To cherish each other

- To grow and evolve together in strength

- To preserve their blessings

- To share their happiness

- To care for their children

- To live long and happy lives together

11

- To remain lifelong partners and friends, making two imperfect halves into one perfect whole.

Socrates, the yogi of ancient Greece, was asked: "Which is better, to marry or not to marry?" In answer, he said, "Whichever you do, you will ultimately repent." He meant to say that marriage is like a *Delhi ka laddu, khayega to bhi pachtayega, nahi khayega to bhi pachtayega.* Whether you marry or whether you do not marry – both ways you will repent.

On another occasion when he was asked the same question "Which is better, to marry or not to marry?" he answered, "By all means, marry. If you get a good wife you will become very happy. But if you get a bad one, you will become a philosopher – and that is good for any man."

He himself did not get a good wife. Xanthippe was her name. She troubled her husband, again and again. One day, in anger, she abused her husband, and out of her lips flowed a stream of coarse invectives. Socrates quietly left the house. When Xanthippe found that her husband was gone, she took up a bucket of dirty water and threw it on him as he walked underneath the balcony of their house. The good man that he was, he looked up and said, "Formerly it thundered, now it pours!"

Why The Hindu Ideal Of Marriage Is Unique

It is said that Plato put forward the theory that each soul was created with two complementary aspects – male and female. The 'whole' soul so created was then split up into its male and female halves before human incarnation. Therefore, Plato emphasises, human beings spend their lives yearning for the ideal union with their 'soul-mate' – a longing which, for some people, is never fulfilled!

The Hindu ideal is slightly different. Here, man and woman represent two aspects of the divine – as portrayed in the dual deity *Ardhanarishwar*. It is as if the Lord Himself has declared that the female is an equal, indispensable aspect of human life. Thus, there is no question of inferiority or superiority. Physically, emotionally, temperamentally, men and women are undoubtedly different. But one is incomplete without the other.

The Hindu marriage is not based on mutual attraction or mere self-interest. Shakespeare talks of the ideal marriage as "the marriage of true minds". The Hindu marriage may be described as the union of *two families*. In this union, there is no room for petty ambitions and personal ego-trips. What is involved is love for the entire family that one is marrying into. The maintenance of domestic peace and harmony and the skillful management of social relationships is the sacred duty of every Hindu woman. When she cultivates love, affection and a strong sense of duty for the entire family, she becomes the power and force that cements family relationships together, and prevents the family from emotional break-up.

Someone remarked the other day, that the term 'joint family' has now taken on a new meaning. If husband, wife and child are living together, this indeed is a 'joint family' by today's standards; for the sad fact is that homes are breaking up so rapidly that single parents, divorced couples and children without a sense of identity and belonging, have now ever increasingly become the norm. If husbands and wives cannot live in peace and harmony with their own offspring, what becomes of old people? Who is to care for aged grandparents and old parents?

The ideal Hindu marriage insists that the newly married couple should work together for the welfare of the family.

Success in marriage is much more than finding the right person. I find myself rather amused when I hear young people talk about finding Mr. Right or Miss Right and the 'chemistry' that will ignite a spark when they come across the 'right' person...

Love must not be confounded with physical sensation or sexual attraction. These are not enough to make a marriage successful. That is why I urge my young friends not to *fall* in love – but *rise* in true love!

It was a wise man who said, "In marriage, *being* the right person is far more important than finding the right person."

Marriage is not meant to be just a means to satisfy one's carnal desires. In its highest form, it enables a man and woman to seek spiritual perfection in each other's company, promoting and supporting their quest for life's fulfilment.

Marriage is also fundamental to civilised society, for it promotes communities, develops lineage and links the past with the future, by encouraging parents and children to perpetuate the family traditions with *shraddha* (devotion).

This does not mean that the young couple who enter into wedlock are paragons of perfection. Perfection in relationships is created through conscious and deliberate effort. So-called 'incompatibilities' and 'misunderstandings' have to be resolved through continual effort, understanding and reconciliation – by a constant process of loving and forgiving, give and take.

Marriage is much more than a love-affair based on mutual passion or physical attraction. Such a 'loveaffair' only promotes selfish pleasure. When this pleasure wears thin, cracks begin to appear and the marriage begins to fall apart.

I do not agree with today's constant harping on mutual incompatibility. I think it is a myth invented by lawyers so that they may be able to argue in favour of divorce. There is no such thing as emotional incompatibility. There are only misunderstandings and mistakes which can easily be set right if we have the will to do so.

Marriage is not just an institution, it is a sacrament, a sacred union. It was after centuries of experience that the wise ones of ancient times formulated the rules of marriage. Nowadays we have chaos in society. There is no respect for the sanctity of marriage. Just as there are traffic laws, which have to be followed to avoid accidents, similarly there are laws of marriage. When you get married, your life is regulated by certain rules. Freedom is not doing what you like. Freedom is the ability to do what you ought to do and should do.

I have said repeatedly, I do *not* believe in divorce. I believe marriage is a sacrament. It must not be broken, because that interferes with the law of *karma*.

Marriage is commitment for life. It is a permanent, lifelong relationship. Obviously, such a longstanding bond will bring with it, its share of joys and sorrows, pain and pleasure. True love bears all, endures all and triumphs! It is very common to see people in India celebrating their silver and golden wedding anniversaries, for people still continue to cherish the divinity of marriage and its ideal of lifelong commitment.

Choosing The Right Partner

If a marriage is to last and be successful in every sense of the word, it must be based on harmony, which does not depend on external things alone. Much more important than outward appearance is the nature, the temperament of a person. One's true colours are revealed when people start living together after marriage. But the important thing is *not* to be misled by appearances and misjudge the character of the person you are going to marry.

A girl came to me and said, "There is this boy whom I wish to marry."

"Tell me about him," I said to her.

"He belongs to an aristocratic family," she said.

"That is zero," I said to her.

"He holds a doctorate in computer science."

"Another zero," I said to her.

"He is the only son, the only child of his parents."

"Yet another zero," I said to her.

"He is so handsome," she continued.

"One more zero," I said.

The zeros went on multiplying until finally, she said, "He is a man with sterling qualities of character and faith in God."

"If that is so," I said to her, "then put one in front of all the zeros and he will score that many marks."

You must study the temperament of the individual and see how far your temperaments will be in harmony with each other.

This is what will make a marriage last.

The fact of the matter is, when you are emotionally involved, you may find it very difficult to judge the character of the individual you love. Therefore, I think it is the duty of parents to make adequate inquiries and verify the facts about the person.

I am often asked the question: Which is better, an arranged marriage or love marriage?

My answer surprises everyone. I always tell them, "Love marriage or marriages fixed by parents – all marriages are arranged by God."

I firmly believe that in the beautiful book of life that is bestowed upon us by God, there are *three important pages* on which He has already written whatever is to be written. On these three pages – these three aspects of life – we have no choice; or rather, our choice has already been made for us. These three aspects are:

1) When, where and in which family you are born.

2) When, where and whom you shall marry.

3) When, where and how you shall die.

Many of my friends find this difficult to understand. "But Dada," they argue, "I have made it very clear to my parents that my marriage is going to be a matter of my choice and mine alone! *I* shall choose whom I marry, and *I* shall decide how and when and where I get married."

In fact, quite a few young people are so particular about this that they look hard for Mr. or Miss Right, and decide upon their own life partners, without the parents' 'interference'. It appears to all intents and purposes that they have definitely exercised their right to choose in this crucial aspect of life.

Yes – they have exercised their choice but not in the manner that they think they have. Let me explain.

When a man reaches the world of the gods after his death, he is given the opportunity to look backward and forward in time, glimpsing the great Cosmic Plan and the part he has to play in the plan – in his past and future lives. This enables him to prepare for the next earth incarnation. In the utterly peaceful and tranquil atmosphere of this world of the gods, the soul formulates its plan for its next earthly life. It is here that we ourselves write down our destiny. It is here that each individual *chooses* the spouse who will help him/her to evolve and grow in the next earth-life. This is why I say, all marriages have been 'arranged' as per the Law of *Karma*. We have already made this choice. This is what is meant by the saying, "Marriages are made in Heaven." How can we then reject what we have chosen for our own good? How can divorce ever be acceptable under such circumstances?

The ideal is that every husband should treat his wife as a queen. Theodore Roosevelt, one of the distinguished Presidents of the United States, when he was a student at Harvard, fell in love with a 17-

year old girl, Alice. It was what they call love at first sight. In due course, they were married. And an entry in Theodore Roosevelt's diary reads, "Now that I have won the hand of Alice, the aim of my whole life shall be to make her happy, to shield her and guard her from every trial. And oh, how I will cherish my sweet queen! How she, so pure and sweet and beautiful, can think of marrying me, I cannot understand, but I praise and thank God it is so!"

I recall the words of a wise man, Joseph Fort Newton. He said, "The happiest wife is not the one who marries the best man but the one who makes the best of the man she marries."

Men and women were created by God so that they could form one complete whole. So it is that He endowed men with certain qualities and women with complementary qualities. By themselves neither men nor women are complete. Men have strength, determination, energy, vigour and guts. Women have great sensitivity, spiritual aspirations, the spirit of sympathy, service and sacrifice. Men rely on their intellect. Women have intuition. Rudyard Kipling said, "A woman's guess is much more accurate than a man's certainty." Man and woman together form one

24

complete person. By themselves both are incomplete. Each needs the other. Each has to learn much from the other. A holy man said, "Except a man become a woman he cannot enter the Kingdom of Heaven. And except a woman become a man she cannot enter the Kingdom of Heaven."

Love may begin with physical attraction but marriage, in due course, fuses them together so that they form one complete whole. This is the purpose of marriage. When we forget it, we lose the proper perspective of marriage.

I am afraid, today there are so many couples who may be classified as married strangers. They may share the same house, the same table, the same car and yet may actually be drifting away from each other.

The Great Value Of
Grihasta Ashrama

In the *Gospel of Sri Ramakrishna* there are several sections entitled 'Advice to Householders'. This just goes to show the great importance that Sri Ramakrishna Parmahansa attached to marriage and home. When we speak about the *grihasta ashrama*, let us not forget that we are talking about over 90% of the population who belong to this category. We find Sri Ramakrishna passing on valuable advice to his devotees about the duties of a *grihasta*.

In those days – perhaps even now – these people tended to undervalue themselves. Many of them would tell Sri Ramakrishna, "After all, we are only *grihastas* : what can we achieve?" or "We are only *grihastas* : how can we hope to attain God?"

The Saint's answer was simple, "Why can you not attain God? He is the *Antaryami* – the inner ruler who is within each one of us. Think of Him constantly in your daily life as you do your work. You will find that He will take care of you!"

The *grihasta* is one who lives in a *griha* or home. The first thing he must realise is that this home is not a prison! It is a household. When does a home become a prison – you may ask. It becomes a veritable prison when the people living in it restrict their lives, confine their minds to "I" and "Mine." "Get rid of I and Mine," Sri Ramakrishna told the *grihastas* repeatedly. When we are trapped in this narrow circle of egoism and selfishness, we lose the sense of the vastness and magnificence of the Universe of which we are a part. We lose the sense of dignity and responsibility that is attached to the great *grishasta* ashrama.

The *Manusmriti* tells us, "The *grihasta ashrama* is the greatest among the *ashramas* because it is only the *grihasta* who provides food and education to the people of the other three *ashramas.*"

As I explained earlier, the *grihasta* in productive work, earns money and supports the entire society. In fact, society survives on the strength of the *grihastas*. Why then should a *grihasta* underestimate

27

himself? Why should he doubt his ability to attain God?

What Manu said all those centuries earlier, makes sense in the totally different context of today: the *grihasta* is the ideal citizen of the society. When you say 'citizen' you are obviously talking about someone who is not concerned only with his home and his family. He or she is deeply concerned with the progress of the society and the country. Only when this ideal is held before him does he become a true citizen. So it is with a *grihasta* : he will be imprisoned in his home if his vision is not broadened, if his mind is not opened to his duties and responsibilities.

There are two values attached to the *grihasta* as to a citizen. The first is freedom. In the modern era, we are proud of the fact that we are all free citizens. But what many of us forget is that responsibility goes hand in hand with freedom.

In the Hindu tradition, several great *avatars* appeared in the *grihasta ashrama* to give dignity, prestige and strength to the Hindu ideal of marriage. These *avatars* not only enhanced the glory of marriage, they also served as wonderful examples to householders.

28

To be a true *grihasta* one must cherish the institution of marriage, and one must develop selfconfidence and self-reliance. We must stop constantly devaluing ourselves by saying, "I am only a *grihasta*. I am only a *samsari* – I am tied down by my bonds." No! Cast aside such doubts, strengthen your mind, broaden your vision, and vow to contribute to the betterment of your culture, your community, your society, your country and the world you live in! This is your prerogative as a *grihasta*, a true citizen!

How may we shed the feeling of regret, confinement associated with being a *grihasta* ? Here again, Sri Ramakrishna has the answer – Live in *samsara* (the world), but don't allow *samsara* (worldliness) to live in you. He gives us the example of the boat and urges that the boat must be on the waters – but the water must not be in the boat else the boat will sink and we all will be drowned. The new *grihastas* of the new millennium can learn from the Saint of Dakshineshwar how to make their married life glorious – by working together as enlightened citizens in a spirit of love and service.

I am deeply saddened when I hear a woman say, "I am only a housewife." What she expresses in these words is the regret that she is not a working woman, not a professional, but someone confined to the four walls of the home. She does not know her real dignity and worth! If only she realises her onerous duties and responsibilities as a builder of the home, as the shaper of a new generation, as the architect of a new India, she would not refer to herself in such belittling terms!

The Five *Yajnas* Of A Householder

Hindu *dharma* enjoins a *grihasta* to perform five different kinds of *yajna* or sacrifices. In the Hindu way of life a *yajna* is not a physical or material sacrifice – it is a course of action that has a purificatory effect on life. A *yajna* performed in the right spirit helps one to be free from impurities of the mind and heart. Negative impulses and destructive thought patterns such as anger, greed, envy, jealousy, and hatred are utterly destroyed, when the mystical fire is kindled in the heart within.

What are the five *yajnas* expected of the *grihasta*?

Deva yajna or worship of God. We invoke our *ishta devta* in prayer. We utter *mantras, shlokas*, sing *kirtan* in His praise.

There are several Gods and Goddesses in the Hindu Pantheon, and each one has special days, special festivals, special occasions to be remembered. It does not matter whom you choose – for all of them are manifestations of the One *Brahman*.

Lord Krishna tells us in the *Gita,* "May you satisfy the Gods by the performance of sacrifice. In turn, may the Gods, thus satisfied, enhance your fulfilment."

This is nothing but an appeal to dedicate our life and actions to God. The implication is that we should rise above the low satisfaction of living life on the sensory level alone. We cease to become self-centred, and grow in the life of light. Your thoughts, words and deeds focus upon the Divine within you. Your consciousness expands, and you begin to taste true inner joy.

Performing *Deva yajna* contributes not only to your own peace and happiness – it works for the welfare of the world at large.

Rishi yajna – involves studying the wisdom of our ancient *rishis* – in other words, reading our great scriptures and drawing wisdom and inspiration from them for our daily life. Alas, very few people are aware of the vast spiritual treasures enshrined in the *Vedas* and *Upanishads*. The *Gita* alone is a repository of profound insights and valuable teachings that will help you to live a life that integrates head, hand, heart, and spirit. When you imbibe this valuable knowledge and share it with others, you not only make your life more meaningful, you are also passing on the wisdom of the ancients to future generations.

Pitru yajna -- or special rites for our forefathers. The soul of our ancestors may be abiding in various subtle planes, according to their *karma*. It is the duty of every householder to remember them and offer special prayers or acts of service in their memory, for their *mukti* or liberation.

This may be a ritual or *shraddha* in traditional households, performed on the death-anniversary of the departed dear ones. In other homes, this may be done as an act of service to the needy and underprivileged. Whichever you choose, perform the same with faith and devotion so that the souls of your ancestors may rejoice and bless you.

Above all remember, that everything you do and say reflects on the family to which you belong. Nothing you do must detract from your good name. This will enhance the glory of your ancestors and make them proud of you.

Manushya yajna – or actions performed for the good of other human beings. This involves all actions born of compassion and charity – such as feeding the hungry, bringing medical aid to the sick, helping the aged and lightening the burden of those in pain.

As I have said repeatedly, the One God dwells in all human beings. When you serve your brother or sister in love, you serve God. So did my beloved Master tell us, "Service of the poor is worship of God."

Bhuta yajna – consists of your duties and responsibilities to non-human forms of life – to all creatures that breathe the breath of life. "Birds and animals," Sadhu Vaswani said, "are our brothers and sisters in the One family of creation." It is our duty to protect them and care for their well-being.

We are evolving into a new consciousness, a new attitude to environmental concerns. We have grown in the awareness that plants, trees, birds, animals, fishes and insects are all part of the great ecosystem that sustains life. They maintain the ecological balance that is vital for our healthy living on this planet.

Hindu culture enjoins us to perform acts of

kindness to animals. Thus we honour cows, offer 'worship' to trees on days like *Vata Poornima* and offer milk to snakes on *Nag Panchami*. The *tulsi* is considered sacred – and *ahimsa* is enjoined upon all of us, that we may abstain from all food of violence.

By performing the five *yajnas*, it is believed, we fulfil debts to the Gods, to the *rishis*, to the ancestors, to humanity at large, and the wonderful world we live in.

Ultimately this reinforces the ideal that you are a part of this Universe, you are an instrument in God's Divine plan for the world. You are an aspect of the Divine yourself. You are led to the cosmic vision of the *Vedas* – the vision of the One-in-All, which is the essence of the scriptures. As this vision grows, you too move towards liberation from the cycle of birth and death.

The Spiritual Ideals Of Marriage

Modern genetics emphasises the concept of human uniqueness. Our genetic inheritance ensures that certain attributes have been passed on to us from our parents. But we have a far more valuable inheritance that sets us apart from animals – our cultural and spiritual inheritance. We belong to a great culture with a rich legacy of literature, art, religion, and philosophy – a valuable legacy that must be preserved, protected, indeed enhanced, to be passed on to generations after our own. We are not only passing on our hereditary biological system to our children; we are passing on the cultural inheritance which goes back to the *Vedas!* This is the great responsibility of the *grihasta!*

When a wife or a husband confines herself or himself to the four walls of the home, and is concerned only with his/her genetic family, then indeed the home becomes a prison. To such a narrow-minded, constricted person will apply the belittling description, "...only a *grihasta*."

I would stress again and again the immortal truth of the sanctity of the spirit – *Tat twam asi!* That art Thou! You are the divine, immortal *atman!*

The *rishis* of ancient India have taught us that there are three kinds, three levels of energy: *bahubalam* or physical energy; *buddhibalam* or intellectual energy, *atmabalam* or spiritual energy, which is truly tremendous and beyond compare! This is what we must aim to cultivate, through the right practise of the duties and responsibilities of *grihasta ashrama*.

Anatomy, physiology and neurology can tell us about the body; even modern psychology has not progressed enough to help us understand the human mind in all its complexity. As for what lies beyond the mind – western science and knowledge have no means to unravel the mysteries of the *atman*. This is where Hindu culture and tradition score over all the rest.

I have spoken at length on these issues to under-score an important point about the married state. *Grihasta ashrama* has two dimensions – the worldly and the spiritual. In the early part of marriage, in your youth, you will find yourselves engaged in work, livelihood, earning money, getting a job, raising your children, building your reputation, and good name in society. But side by side with this achievement – oriented drive, we also need to build on *atmabalam* or spiritual strength.

The Six Enemies Of Humanity

Ancient Indian scriptures speak of *sadripu* – the six enemies of a human being. These are not outside us, they are within! Therefore, conquering these enemies within is truly a self-conquest, which is achieved only through *sadhana*, self-discipline and self-control.

What are these six enemies?

1. *kama* – unrestrained lust
2. *krodha* – anger, which burns you if you do not burn it
3. *lobha* – unmitigated greed
4. *moha* – delusion that is born of ignorance
5. *mada* – pride
6. *mathsarya* – envy or malice

These are the negative forces within us that can destroy us spiritually if we do not vanquish them.

The body is strong; the senses *(indriyas)* are powerful. But the mind *(manas)* is above them. Beyond and higher than the mind is the discriminatory faculty *(buddhi)* that helps us know right from wrong and beyond it all is the *atman* – the Spirit.

Truly, every householder will evolve into a wonderful citizen, when he realizes the need to conquer the enemy within. This awareness is reached, when he realises the power of the spirit! The householder's life cannot be complete, cannot be truly happy, unless there is spiritual growth.

Evolving Together – Spiritually

Grow together spiritually – this is my advice to all young married couples. 'Individuals' will collide; they are in conflict with other 'individuals'. But wellrounded, well-developed 'personalities' do not clash. Sri Ramakrishna distinguished between unripe and ripe mangoes – between unripe individuals who are unable to escape the narrow confines of the 'I' and 'Mine' and those that have evolved spiritually and become truly human. If husband and wife remain unripe, the home will be reduced to a site of conflict and tension. When they become ripe the home will be a temple of peace and harmony.

Spiritual energy – *atmabalam* – manifests itself as values in human life like love, compassion and the spirit of service. This is the secret of true growth. This is what our scriptures call *adhyatmika vikasa* – spiritual development. When this goal is kept in mind, *grihasta ashrama* will indeed become a

41

wonderful experience. India and the world, will benefit from the *grihasta ashrama*.

Whenever I am requested to conduct an engagement ceremony, I suggest that both the boy and the girl should vow to respect, cherish and promote the spiritual aspirations of the other, and not stand in the way of such aspirations. Let me make it clear, this applies to both husband and wife. Many people are apt to imagine that it is the men, the husbands who have religious or spiritual inclinations, while their wives/women are intolerant or insensitive about such inclinations and tend to distract them and disrupt their spiritual activities. This is not true. Women, I have always believed, possess great *atmashakti*or spiritual strength. They, too, have their own spiritual aspirations which their husbands must learn to respect.

It is not without reason that women are given such importance in Hindu culture and tradition. The woman is the transmitter of tradition from one generation to another. The woman is the centre of the home – the *grihalakshmi*. As a mother, she sows seeds of character and idealism in her children.

42

Therefore as my beloved Master, Sadhu Vaswani said:

"The woman-soul has the *shakti* to rebuild the shattered world in the strength of her intuitions, her purity, her simplicity, her spiritual aspiration, her sympathy and silent sacrifice. The woman-soul will lead us upward, on!"

Many spiritual elders and teachers will tell you that they have often found a great level of spiritual awareness in married couples – greater than the awareness one finds in people who are leading monastic lives or lives of renunciation. I myself know of many married men and women who practise spirituality in their daily life, within the *ashrama* of marriage. They work actively to fulfil their worldly responsibilities and also fulfil their commitments to the larger family circle, including parents, childrenand others. They lead full lives, and also give of themselves in selfless service. And they resolutely and sincerely pursue the path of spiritual growth. How wonderful and admirable this is! How beneficial to society and culture!

This is possible for every man and woman who enters the *grihasta ashrama* – provided they realise

43

their responsibilities as spouses, parents and citizens. When they enter into the true spirit of the *grihasta ashrama* as it is outlined in the scriptures, when they accept their onerous duties and responsibilities and challenges as stepping stones to their own spiritual growth, then they will find that marriage is indeed a spiritually fulfilling commitment.

Four Purposes Of Life

As I said to you, the *Vedas* have outlined a fourfold purpose for human life – *dharma*, *artha*, *kama* and *moksha*.

In an ideal marriage, the couple's life must be rooted in *dharma* – ethical values. Without compromising these values, they should establish meaningful human relationships (*kama*) and secure their financial assets (*artha*). This should be utilised to promote *dharma* and move towards the ultimate goal of *moksha* (liberation).

In the material world we live in, it is easy for people to lose sight of the higher goals, and to consider *kama* and *artha* as absolute ends in themselves. But you must remember, when sense pleasures and the acquisition of wealth are made the focus of your life, it will lead to a terrible sense of imbalance, resulting in personal grief, loss and frustration.

Let me explain that. If you seek wealth through dishonest means, that wealth will bring you no peace. If you seek lustful, illicit relationships, you will never attain the happiness you seek. Money can change your life, it is true – but not necessarily for the better! Pleasures will lull you into a sense of false content – but not for long!

The ancient scriptures tell us the story of the King Yayati who lived a long and full life. But when he noticed the first grey hair on his head, he was worried that all his pleasures would cease soon. The future did not seem appealing. If only he could be younger!

In desperation, Yayati turned to his sons and asked them if any one of them would accept his age and offer him their youth instead. Not surprisingly, they all refused – except one, who was detached, dispassionate and felt compassion for his pleasureseeking father. "I will be glad to exchange my youth for your old age," the young man told Yayati.

It was accomplished and Yayati returned to a life of active pleasure and indulgence.

But time flew past and once again, Yayati could not escape the onset of old age. Then it was that he realised that worldly desires and sensual pursuits would only lead to a craving for more and more. There would never be a real sense of satisfaction or contentment.

Truly has the sage Bhartrahari said, "Craving does not age, it does not decay, but we ourselves continue to decay."

Raja Bhartrahari was a great man in every sense of that term. He was a just and merciful king. He was good to everyone. Verily, he was a model king.

One day, they brought to him an *amarphal* – the fruit of immortality – and said to him, "O king, this fruit is the only one of its kind. We have brought it to you because you are the one person who deserves to live for ever and ever more."

Bhartrahari accepted the fruit. But as he was about to eat it, he said to himself, "Of what use is life to me without my beloved? Let me give this *amarphal* to my wife, whom I love more than my life. Let her live for ever and ever more."

So the king passed the *amarphal* to his wife saying, " This is the fruit of immortality, eat it, and you, my beloved, will never die."

The queen accepted the fruit. But as destiny would have it, she was secretly in love with the coachman.

47

She said to herself, "Of what use will this fruit be to me if I live on, but my dear coachman perishes?"

So she passed on the fruit to the coachman.

As for the coachman, he was in love with a prostitute. He handed over the fruit to the prostitute.

In a moment of rare introspection, the prostitute said to herself, "Of what use is life to me? The longer I live, the more sins I commit and the more I drag other people into a life of sinfulness. If there is anyone who deserves to live eternally, it is our great, good and just king, Raja Bhartrahari."

So back came the *amarphal* to Raja Bhartrahari.

The king was amazed, he was dumbfounded! How did the fruit get into the hands of this prostitute? He made inquiries. He found that his wife had been unfaithful to him.

"What a fool I was to have placed my trust in the world and in a creature of this world!" he said to himself. "Let me lay all my trust in Him who never faileth. Let me set out in quest of the One and only One Beloved, the First and the Only Fair, the Purest of the Pure, the Spotless, the Stainless."

His life was changed. He was born anew. Renouncing his kingdom, he became a *jignasu*, a seeker of truth.

It was a wise philospher who said, "Life is like a house. Without *dharma*, the house has no foundation. Without *artha*, it has no walls. Without *kama*, it has no furnishings. Without *moksha*, it has no roof."

I urge you to adopt a wholesome plan of living, in which the ideal of *dharma* is not compromised while you pursue the other goals. But do not forget, *artha* and *kama* are but means to an end – our ultimate destination of *moksha*, liberation from the cycle of birth and death.

What Next?

Everyone talks about goals and objectives these days. But, I am afraid that many young people today limit themselves to material goals.

A distinguished educationist was travelling from New Delhi to Chennai by train. His co-passenger was a young boy who was delighted to share with him a creditable success that he had achieved recently. He had gained admission to the prestigious Indian Institute of Technology – IIT, Madras. He was elated, he was ecstatic, his future was ensured; he was *made!*

Gently, the educationist began to question the young boy about his plans for the future. What did he plan to do after IIT?

"Go to the States of course," said the boy confidently. "I'll seek admission to one of the top universities. A US degree will work wonders for my career."

"After that?"

The boy smiled smugly. "I'll try my best to settle in the US. If that is not possible, well, I shall work for a multinational in India." He added, "This country may not be America, but it has its plus points. With a five-figure salary, one can live like a king here!"

"What next?"

The boy smiled self-consciously. "My parents will help me find a rich and beautiful girl. I know parents will queue up to find a good match such as the one I hope to be! The girl is sure to come loaded with money, jewels and other property. What more can I ask for?"

"What then?" persisted the older man.

Now, the boy was becoming bored. "You know very well sir, what should follow. A big house, car, lavish lifestyle, holidays abroad, clubs, parties..."

"What then?"

"Oh, I suppose there will be children..." and the boy sat up with sudden resolve. "And I shall work hard, earn all the money I can to give my children the best of everything!"

"What then?"

"My children will go abroad for their higher studies, and I will find brilliant matches for them – nothing short of the best!"

What then? *Tateh kim* ?

Is there nothing more to life than cars, houses, fat incomes and that which money can buy? Can this be the overall goal of one's life – thus far and no further?

I am sure you will all agree that we need to have higher aims, more worthwhile goals than that! Therefore I urge all young men and women to ask themselves why they wish to get married – and let me also steer them in the direction of an appropriate answer. If you decide to get married, it must be to help each other fulfil the highest goal – spiritual evolution and ultimately, self-realisation that leads to God-realisation.

The Path Of Marriage

There is a story narrated to us in the *Mahabharata* which emphasises the greatness of marriage.

A Brahmin *tapasvi* who had successfully conquered the senses and passions, was seated in the shade of a tree, performing his daily austerities. A bird sitting on the branch of the tree happened to drop its excreta on to his head at that moment. Startled, he opened his eyes and gazed in anger at the bird. Such was the power of his *tapasya* that the bird dropped down dead before him, burnt down and reduced to ashes! He was grieved at the death of the bird, but amazed at his own power. It actually made him feel very egotistical and superior that he had acquired such power through his own efforts.

Shortly afterwards, he entered a nearby village where he wished to seek *biksha* (alms) as was his wont. He was used to women rushing out to touch his feet, bow down before him and seek his blessings before offering him the best, the choicest food from their homes.

Today, he faced a different experience. He was received with great respect and devotion by a young wife who said to him, "O *tapasvi*, I humbly request you to wait a while, for I am serving my husband at the moment."

Taken aback by the legitimate request, the *tapasvi* waited for sometime, but became angry and impatien that a woman of no consequence was subjecting him to such delay. How dare she neglect him to serve her husband – who was he anyway?

Presently he called out to her in anger, "Look, woman! I have asked you for food and I want it now, because I have no time to waste! I have devoted myself to the Lord and I lead a life of renunciation. It is the duty of a *grihasti* like you to provide me with food.Obviously, you are ignorant of the spiritual power of a *tapasvi*. It can burn you to cinders if you are not careful!"

The woman took her time to complete what she was doing and came out with food for him. Calmly, she said to him, "O *tapasvi*, I did not keep you waiting without good reason. I was only doing my ordained duty, serving my husband with love and devotion. Your anger does you little good. I know you caused a little bird to be burnt to ashes just a while ago. But I am not like that poor bird!"

The *tapasvi* was taken aback by the realisation that she knew all about him, even though she was just an ordinary housewife, as we put it. He fell at her feet humbly. "Thank you mother, for enlightening me," he said. "I have a lot more to learn about life and the world. I now realise that the path you walk as a *grihasti* is as great and valuable as the path I have trod as an ascetic!"

True indeed! The path of marriage and parenthood, of living in the world can also be a path of love and service, of seeking and attaining self-realization. It is not necessarily inferior to other paths that seek God. In fact, marriage is a great institution that helps to teach and establish the values and ideals that will contribute to a good society. Husbands and wives who create a home where peace and serenity prevail, deserve to be credited with great achievement. When children grow up in an atmosphere of love and joy and imbibe good values, these homes contribute to the future of society. When married love matures, it becomes familial love; as familial love evolves, it grows further to encompass the society and community. In its final fulfilment, it achieves the capacity to love all – all people, all creation, all creatures that breathe the breath of life. When we become capable of such selfless, unconditional, undemanding love, surely we have reached the highest state of consciousness!

Making A Marriage Work

How can we ensure a happy marriage?

Some people believe that making money is the best way to ensure a successful marriage. Both men and women fall prey to this fallacy – for it is indeed a false belief to imagine that money can ensure happiness in marriage.

I met a wealthy man who complained to me, "I work hard day and night to provide my family with all the comforts that they need. I have risen to the top of the business world, and I am No. 1 in my sector. My wife has been given everything a woman could wish for, my children go to the best schools and have their every whim and fancy satisfied. Yet they do not appreciate all that I do for them. Tell me, what more can I do for them?"

His wife and children had a ready answer to that question, "Spend more *time* with us!"

They were not happy with the money and comforts he provided for them. They wanted his personal care, his loving attention.

Another husband said to me, "I prefer to stay out of my home most of the time because my wife constantly nags me."

When a woman begins to feel lonely and neglected she tries to draw attention to herself by such negative means. She accuses her husband, makes critical statements about him and starts quarrelling. In this way, she projects her own negative feelings on to him.

I know many men in India who insist that their wives should bow down before them and touch their feet. While this is a beautiful gesture of reverential love, it should not be expected as a matter of right. The man should not regard himself as a superior being to whom the wife can never be an 'equal'.

Several young men and women are obsessed about the educational qualifications and the intellectual abilities of their partners. But marital success is not achieved through parity in degrees. Two intellectuals need not always ensure a happy home. In fact, they might end up arguing constantly as some of our politicians do!

It requires love, commitment, understanding, patience, and forgiveness to make a marriage successful. Both partners must enter into the sanctified relationship understanding its great potential and its deep significance, knowing that they have chosen to live together, to bring out the best in each other and to make each other as happy as possible.

Young people who do not realise this truth enter into marriage with wrong expectations. "Can she/he make me happy?" they ask; while the right question is: "Can I make this person happy? Can we live happily together for the rest of our lives?"

A spontaneous "I love you!" is far more valuable than a demanding, "Do you love me?" The former declares selfless, giving love. The latter is selfish, *taking* love.

Young people must enter into marriage with a serious sense of commitment, integrating head and heart. It is a commitment one makes for a lifetime and not to be taken lightly. When you enter marriage with this sense of commitment, your home is sure to become a temple of love, peace, joy, and harmony – a centre of light amidst the encircling darkness. The love and peace that emanates from such homes reaches out, radiates towards others. The parents and children from these homes have the wonderful ability to love and serve others, and can become the catalysts who transform society.

The Miracle Of Marriage

Every successful, happy marriage is a miracle of love. I know dozens of men and women who are alive today, who have been rescued from near-certain death by the miraculous power of love. Despite the troubled times we live in, it is still very common to come across people who have succeeded in making their marriage work – 'silver' medallists who have completed 25 years, 'goldies' who have crossed the 50-year mark. They are a living testimony to the remarkable fact that marital love can grow, endure and triumph against all odds.

There is, there can be no such thing as a trouble-free marriage. Life brings its share of crises, problems and challenges to everyone of us. The successful marriage not only survives, but flourishes through them. The secret of this success is the selfless love and commitment that can stand the severest tests –

like financial ruin and unexpected illnesses and disease.

You have no doubt heard the story of King Midas who was granted the boon of a single wish. You know too, that he asked that all he touched should turn to gold, and the disastrous consequences that followed.

Now let me ask each one of you – if you could have one such boon granted to you, what would you wish for? Health? Wealth? Long life? Happiness?

Midas thought that the prospect of permanent wealth would ensure happiness. As it happened, he was left all alone, in misery – surrounded by glittering riches, but starving to death. The people who could have given meaning to the gold – the members of his family – had been rendered lifeless by the mere touch of his hands, turned into useless gold.

What would you wish for? If you wished for long life, you will surely require someone to share it with. If you wished for good health, you will surely need some one to rejoice in your well-being. If, like Midas, you wished for personal riches, you will surely require someone to enjoy your material treasures with you.

When you have a happy and successful marriage you will be free of the need to wish for anything because you will have someone who is ready to share everything with you!

This is what I call the miracle of marriage: two people who do not take each other for granted, but do take it for granted that they will love and cherish each other all their lives, and give that love priority over everything else in their life. Anybody can laugh together, but a loving husband and wife can cry together.

To laugh, to cry, to work, and to love and live together – each for the other – is surely the most remarkable achievement that two human beings can accomplish. Thus a true marriage is a miracle that defies all the vicissitudes of the crass and selfish world we live in today.

"Where has love gone?" tragic poets wail. "Where has the glory fled?" "Where is the love that I felt all those days ago?"

A happily married woman who celebrated her sixtieth wedding anniversary said to a writer who was interviewing her, "Nobody can find love if they go looking for it alone."

Love is not out there somewhere. It is with you, within you. You and your partner can make it flourish in your marriage. A miracle marriage is within the grasp of all couples who wish to give and take, understand, love, forgive, care, and share. Your wish for the miracle of lasting love can come true when you enter married life in this spirit.

Here are the "Vows of A Miracle Marriage" penned by best-selling author Paul Pearsall, Ph.D.:

We promise to cherish our sacred time together, and to put our marital moments before all others.
(Taking Time for Two)

We promise to learn about and with each other forever.
(Tolerating Confident Uncertainty)

We promise to be as and for our one
(Loving as One)

We promise to look at each other for and with love
(Looking with Love)

We promise to accept our differences to make us stronger together
(Complementing our Spouse)

We promise never to let time or space separate us
(Loving Everywhere Anytime)

64

We promise to accept, tolerate and grow with the chaos of our life

(Caring Through the Chaos)

We promise to see our sadness as symbolic of the intensity of our looking

(Sharing Our Disappointments)

We promise to explore realities of our spirit far beyond what we can see and touch

(Creating Our Own Realities of Love)

And we promise to create a growing, loving energy between us and for the world

(Energising and Being Energised by Our Love)

Modern business management, psychology and medicine make the assumption that selfishness is the ultimate human motivation – the "I", "Me" and "Mine" that Sri Ramakrishna warned us against, if you remember! Such an egotistical approach, such self-centredness, can never make for a happy marriage.

Nobel Prize Laureate Herbert Simon redefines the theory of the 'survival of the fittest' which all of us are familiar with. Dr. Simon observes firmly, "Mother Nature has made sure that nice people still win in the end." According to him, survival of the fittest really means that caring people who understand true love, and are willing to rise above the narrow idea of 'self' for the good of merging with another, are the fittest of all!

Human Relationships : How We May Learn From One Another

I have always believed that life is a school, and experience is our greatest teacher. We enter into various relationships and each one of these is meant to teach us vital truths for our own spiritual evolution. Marriage teaches us mutual respect, mutual love, understanding, tolerance, and a sense of responsibility. Marriage disciplines us, as we learn to be selfless and put others first. Ultimately, love changes us for the better.

Sometime ago I was talking to a group of college teachers. They pointed out to me that school teachers are expected to undergo special training, even acquire a special degree or diploma before they begin to teach. Without a D.Ed (Diploma is Education) or a B. Ed (Bachelor of Education) no school will hire you. College/university teachers on the other hand require no such special qualifications. Fresh out of their

M. Phil or Ph. D they can walk into a B.A. or M.A. class and just hold forth to their students.

A learned man I know, once expressed the opinion that men and women too, should be required to undergo special training before they are allowed to enter marriage and parenthood. They should be emotionally, psychologically and spiritually educated to make their marriages meaningful and enlightened.

Human relationships flounder when mutual respect is lacking. Marriages fail when companionship and understanding are absent in the partners. Therefore, I urge husbands to respect their wives, and wives to respect their husbands. Children should respect parents and parents should respect their children's individuality and independence. Give one another the freedom to be themselves, to express themselves, and assert their unique identity! When there is complete understanding, respect and affection, all marriages become 'love-marriages' in the true sense of the word.

But don't wait for the other to begin the process. Don't sit back and say, "How wonderful it would be if my wife grew in the spirit of understanding!" or "I wish my husband would cultivate the spirit of forgiveness!" Instead, begin with yourself! After all, if you don't change yourself, you can't expect to change the rest of the world!

Harmony In Marriage

In a happy and successful marriage, the husband and wife must seek to bring out the best in each other. After all, they have been brought together in the sacred bonds of marriage according to his Divine Plan. They should therefore help each other grow, evolve and unfold their highest potential. If this is kept in focus as the goal of marriage, love and harmony will prevail in the home. When this is lost sight of, love will soon turn to disillusion, and the partners will fail to get the best out of their marriage.

How can you achieve this ideal of love and harmony? Here are a few simple tips:

★ Do not argue about inferiority and superiority. Husbands and wives must recognise they are equal partners. The husband must not treat his wife like a puppet or an object of possession. The wife must not expect to have her every whim and fancy indulged by the husband. Couples should learn to respect one another and recognise the other's rights. It was a wise man who said, "Householders must understand the difference between humility and humiliation, between loving submission and abject surrender." There must be a congenial environment in the home in which each partner enjoys mutual freedom to evolve.

★ Learn to perform your duty, carry out your responsibilities to the family in the spirit of *karma yoga*, as suggested by the *Gita*. In other words, make of your married life, an offering to the Lord Himself. Whatever it is you may be doing – teaching a child, helping him with his homework, attending to household chores, balancing the budget or attending to guests – let it be done as an act of worship to God, in the spirit of fulfilling your *swadharma* (the duty allotted to you).

★ Learn to recognise God in each other. The ancient scriptures tell us, "Where women are worshipped, there the Gods rejoice." Unfortunately, many men accept this in theory, while in practice, they continue to exploit and degrade their wives.

By 'worship' is meant deep respect and reverence for your partner's soul. As I have said repeatedly, we are not the bodies we wear; our reality is the immortal soul within us. When we cherish this reverence for the soul, we will create an atmosphere of ideal love – a love that is strong in giving, sharing and self-sacrifice; a love that is not threatened by the many accidents and incidents of life; a love that burns bright even in adversity; a love that shines as an ever bright lamp to guide us through the dark nights of life.

When you worship the God in each other you lay a strong and secure foundation for a happy and harmonious marriage.

★ Recognise that the bonds of marriage are sacrosanct. According to Hindu *dharma*, marriage is indissoluble. Make a few compromises, sacrifices, if necessary, to nourish your marriage. When mutual adjustments are made with love, understanding and adaptability, your relationship will be smooth, stable and enduring.

★ Always remain loyal, truthful and faithful to one another; I do not condone 'free' marriages where partners allow each other to do as they please. I must insist that sexual fidelity is vital to preserve the spiritual well-being of your marriage.

★ Realise that every situation, every predicament you face in your marriage is helping you to achieve your goal of self-realisation. When your partner displeases you, you grow in the virtue of patience. When you encounter disappointments, you imbibe the spirit of acceptance. When an offence is committed against you, you grow in the spirit of forgiveness.

★ Do not deceive yourself with the false notion that you would have been better off married to someone else! No matter what kind of a person your spouse is, remember there is a Divine plan, a Divine meaning behind your union. With spiritual insight and love, you can bring about a tremendous transformation in one another!

★ Adapt and adjust. Develop the wonderful qualities of tolerance and flexibility. A little spirit of give and take can bring you great rewards.

★ Avoid negative feelings. Do not imagine the worst. Sri Ramakrishna once narrated a parable about a man who was lying on the roadside. A thief passed by and thought to himself, "He tried to rob someone and was beaten up." A drunkard passed by, and he concluded that the man had too much to drink. A saint passed by and thought, "The man has attained a state of identification with the spirit – and has lost body-consciousness!"

Your imagination can mislead you. When your husband does not smile at you, do not conclude that he has stopped loving you. If your wife seems pre- occupied, do not jump to the conclusion that she is simply ignoring you. If you have a little argument or misunderstanding, do not decide that your marriage is at an end!

★ Realise that your children are your greatest responsibility. They are not toys for you to play with; they are not your future insurance. They are souls whom the Lord has entrusted to your care. Do not pamper or indulge them mindlessly. Blend firmness with affection, discipline with love, to give them a secure and healthy environment where they might grow to absorb the deeper values of life.

Here is a prayer I read somewhere:

Let there be harmony between husband and wife.

Let there be harmony between parents and their children.

Let there be harmony among different relatives.

Let there be harmony among friends.

Let there be harmony among the elements.

Let there be harmony between the earth and the sky.

Let harmony be experienced everywhere!

May God bless you with harmony and peace!

According to ancient Hindu scriptures, an ideal family should have the following qualities:

1. *Asha* (optimism): When family members develop faith in God, they have no need to fear the unknown.

They can look to the future with confidence and joy, for they know that God's Will is being done in their lives. The unknown and the unexpected will not daunt them, for they know they can turn every situation to spiritual advantage.

2. Pratiksha (patient waiting): When you have done your duty well, you can rest assured in the conviction that success will be yours. When you imbibe the virtue of perseverance, you will know that the Divine Hand is always holding you, and guiding you. You will be free from impatience and restlessness.

3. Sangata (good company): Learn to cultivate the company of good friends, well-wishers and wise ones. Avoid contact with those who are likely to bring harmful influences into your family.

Let me also urge you friends, to cultivate the habit of family *satsang*. Invite your relations and neighbours too, to join you in *kirtan*, *bhajans*, and recitations from the scriptures.

4. Sukarma (right action): Perform acts of charity and service. These do not have to always depend on cash and material offerings. Give of yourself. Spread kindness and cheer and optimism wherever you go. You and your family will be richly blessed for it!

5. *Atithya* (hospitality): Hindu scriptures tell us, *Athithi devo bhava*. Our guests are manifestations of the Divine. Welcome visitors to your home with warmth. Greet them cordially and offer them your best hospitality. The Gods smile at you as the guests depart from your home in contentment.

In-Laws : In-Love

I have said that in India young men and women do not just get married to each other – they marry *into* families. I dare say this is true of the West too, though they are far less emotional and far more pragmatic in their approach to the issue. That is, it is understood, taken for granted that young couples who marry will set up homes on their own, visiting their parents only at weekends or on holidays or special occasions. Long visits by parents are not common, and each couple functions independently in their nuclear family unit.

In India, on the other hand, familial bonds are much stronger. Parents' influence – unkind people would say interference – continues to be exerted well into the couple's married life. Many young couples too, continue to make their homes under their parents' roof, still keeping the good old joint family system alive.

I do not wish to speak about the benefits or shortcomings of the joint family. I merely wish to say that East or West, one's ties to parents and siblings are strong and cannot be broken off just because people choose to get married. Our parents brought us into this world, and we owe the gift of life to them. How can a spouse supercede this link? After all, human love is not a mathemathical quantity – if I give you half of it, the others can only share what is left, or some such calculation! The more you love, the more you become capable of loving! Do you, as a couple with three children, give each child only 33.3% of your love, while a couple with two children love their offspring 50% each? The heart has its own vast spaces – and in it, there is room for your spouse, children, parents, siblings, uncles, aunts, cousins, friends – and in-laws!

I have always maintained that I am not happy about the term 'in-law'. No law or statute can force you to become 'mother' and 'father' or 'brother' and 'sister' to a stranger who marries your son or daughter. But love can turn this relationship into one large extended family embracing another. Therefore, I prefer the term *mother-in-love*; *father-in-love*.

A young woman said to her friend, " I dread it when my mother-in-law comes to visit us. I know she's my husband's mother and I am supposed to love her – but she takes over my house, my kids and my life, and tries to manage everything! I can't take it!"

Another sad fact is that mother-in-law jokes and stories are universal. You will hardly find many father-in-law jokes. I wonder why – perhaps it is because women are forced to spend time at home longer.

Friction arises in marriage, when couples cannot handle their in-laws with love. His mother is seen to be domineering and possessive. Her mother is thought to be interfering and intolerant. It is thought that one is disloyal when one voices complaints about them. "Your mother","My mother","Your family","My family" – and the *us* and *our* take a back seat to *yours* and *mine*.

I urge couples to talk to each other about their parents with honesty and frankness. Stop thinking of your parent's family as "them" or "others" – a special and different species from your family. Think of them as human beings with plus and minus points, like your own parents and siblings! Think of them as people – treat them as people!

In this, as in all matters, begin with yourself. If you are patient, loving, kind and understanding, your spouse and your in-laws will love you and appreciate you all the more!

As for parents, I would offer the following suggestions:

1. Learn to let go of your children when they marry. They are entering into a new relationship, a crucial phase of their life, just as you did all those years ago. They are now acquiring new identities, they will now have to make their own decisions. You must learn to stop telling them what to do.

2. When your son/daughter speaks well of the spouse, do not resent it or become envious of the newcomer. Look for something to praise him/her and make your child happy!

3. Appreciate the new situation that emerges – a triangular situation between you, your child and his spouse. It is far more complex, and you must deal with it in a way that will strengthen the bonds of love.

In-laws are *not* outlaws, as one perceptive marriage counsellor remarks. They are ordinary people like you and me, linked up together in a relationship that is both complicated and demanding, when *their* sons and daughters choose to marry someone else's daughters and sons!

Forging new bonds, creating new relationships, is not an easy task. But a little understanding and sensitivity can go a long way to establish loving ties within the extended family. Learn to respect the others' point of view. Make allowances for their preferences and opinions. Try not to become hyper-critical or judgemental. Above all, keep your communication channels open!

To the young couple, I would say:

1. Give each others' parents the love and respect they deserve. You cannot expect your partners to renounce their families just because you are married now.

2. Do not be angry or offensive about your in-laws. Learn to discuss your problems and opinions openly and honestly with your partner. Do it in a good-humoured way.

3. Remember, a person who does not love his own parents cannot be expected to love his wife and children!

The best formula for getting along with your extended family is indeed a time-tested one. Do as you would be done by!

TEN COMMANDMENTS OF MARRIAGE

How may we avoid being married strangers? How may we, after marriage, be fused into one complete whole? So let me pass on to you ten practical suggestions. I sometimes refer to them as the ten commandments of marriage.

First Commandment of Marriage: Avoid the Next Quarrel

If one of you is in a mood to quarrel, the other one should be patient. His or her turn will come at the right time. But both should not be, at the same time, in a mood to quarrel. And even, perchance, if you do quarrel see that you don't let the sun set on the quarrel. And if it so happens that you get up in the middle of the night and quarrel, then don't let the sun rise on your quarrel. Make up before sunset or sunrise. You do not become small if you realise your mistake and go and apologise to your spouse.

There were two people. They celebrated their Golden Anniversary. They said that in all the 50 years that they spent together, they had quarrelled not even once with each other – though both of them were known to have irascible temperaments. They both had the tendency to be angry at the least excuse. They were asked the secret and they said, "The secret is a simple one. When we married, we made a pact with each other that both of us would never lose our temper at the same time. We resolved that if one of us got angry, the other one would be patient. We have held on to that agreement through these 50 years and that is why our marriage has been such a happy one."

I recall the words of the great scientist, Dr. Albert Einstein. When he celebrated his Golden Anniversary, he said: "When we got married, we made a pact with each other. We said that my wife would make all the minor decisions and I would make all the major decisions." And then he added: "The wonder is that in all these 50 years, we have had to make only minor decisions. There has been no occasion to make even one major decision."

All of us hate disagreement and dissension. But they are inevitable in any human relationship. When we disagree – or agree to differ, as the euphemism goes – we are expressing our individuality and independence. How boring the world would be if all of us thought alike!

Therefore, there is no need for husbands and wives to conform to each other, think like each other or indeed become similar to each other! Rather, these differences must be cherished and accepted as opportunities to learn more and more about your spouse – and, in the process, reach a better understanding of yourself.

"The true object of war is peace," observes a wry Chinese philosopher. Disagreement and conflict are unavoidable in marriage. But every effort made to resolve the dissension works ultimately to make the marriage stronger and more secure. This is what marriage counsellors call "constructive disagreement."

There was a saint whose wife was short-tempered and querulous. No matter what he said or did, there were daily battles in the home. However, the saint took it all in his stride. "God be praised for giving me such a wife," he would say. "She is a constant source of inspiration to me to cultivate the spirit of *vairagya* (dispassion) in my heart. I don't even have to go to a *guru* to learn it. I can get it right here in my own home!"

Have you ever watched two children quarrelling? Usually, they fight over very insignificant things, but they get quite heated up about it. Their quarrel proceeds thus:

"How stupid you are!"

"You're stupid too!"

"But not as stupid as you!"

"Go away. I don't want to talk to you ever again."

However, that threat does not really materialise.

Should you return to the 'site of the quarrel' sometime later, you are sure to find the two angry adversaries amicably engaged together in the next game. They are sure to have forgotten the whole unpleasant episode. There is no ill-will, no nursing of grudges, no ego, no brooding, no blame, no judgement, no recriminations! That is what I would call a 'healthy' quarrel – a brief, honest exchange of angry feelings, followed by a brief 'cooling off ' period and then, all is forgiven and forgotten!

This is something we can all learn from children – to be more tolerant and forgiving. Unfortunately, adults specialise in massive egos, holding grudges and displaying unforgiving natures.

Have I told you the story of two men who met at a bar? They realised that they had gone to the same school as children, and were delighted to renew their friendship. What with reliving past memories and catching up on people they knew, time fled, until one man realised with shock that it was close to midnight.

"It's been wonderful meeting you my friend," he said, getting up to leave rather reluctantly. "I wish I could stay on – but I'd better go home soon or my wife will get historical."

"Historical?" said the friend, puzzled. "Don't you mean hysterical?"

"No, I meant historical," laughed the other. "She will go back into the past, delve into the annals of our marriage and recount all my past mistakes and failings."

A razor-sharp memory is a very good thing – but not when it is used to carry around memories of past wrongs.

Many husbands and wives take great pleasure in winning arguments, coming out on top in a quarrel. They often have an unyielding sense of what is right and what is wrong. They are determined to win every 'battle' and if they fail to do so, they actively begin to plot their revenge.

I would give them Gandhiji's words, which he had inscribed on the wall of his room at Sevagram:

> When you are in the right you do not need to lose your temper; when you are in the wrong, you cannot afford to lose it.

This is what the Greek philosopher Epictetus suggests, to overcome the tendency to quarrel: tell yourself that you will not be angry today; then tell yourself that you will not lose your temper for two days together; then three days; then four days....When you have passed 30 days without quarrelling, offer thanks to God.

"Be like the bamboo," a Buddhist teacher tells us. "It is strong on the outside, soft and open on the inside. Its roots are firmly planted in the ground, but firmly intertwined with others for mutual support and strength. The stalk blows freely in the wind, bending rather than resisting. That which bends, rarely breaks."

My advice to young couples is that they can handle frustration and pressure better, by yielding rather than resistance. When you become rigid and inflexible, you insist on seeing things as only black or white. This hampers mutual understanding, and isolates you in your hardened stance. After all, *giving in* does not imply *giving up*. When you yield a little, you will gain, more than you ever dreamt!

A couple was taking a leisurely stroll in the woods, gathering flowers. As they strolled away in opposite directions, they parted ways, meeting each other at a clearing in which stood an impressive statue of a knight. They gazed in admiration at the magnificent statue, one on each side of the statue.

"Look at that shield!" exclaimed the husband. "It is made of pure gold."

"Are you blind?" sneered the wife. "Anyone can see it is made of silver."

"How dare you contradict me, you stupid woman!" roared the husband.

"You are the only one who fails to see how intelligent I am," retorted the wife. "You are prejudiced and blind."

A heated quarrel ensued. But fortunately, it was interrupted by a little girl who ran in between them. "What are you fighting over, aunty and uncle?" she asked. "I heard your quarrel a great distance away."

"Your aunty is so stupid that she cannot see that the shield is golden," said the husband.

"And your uncle is so blind that he does not know the difference between gold and silver," said the wife.

"It's gold!" roared the man.

"It's silver!" screamed the woman.

"Look carefully, aunty and uncle," said the little girl. "Uncle, come over to aunty's side, and you will see that the shield is silver. And if you look at it from uncle's side, aunty, you will realise that it is gold, after all!"

Sheepishly, the couple crossed over to look from the other side, and found that the shield was golden on one side, silver on the other.

"You are both right – but you were both wrong to fight about it," laughed the little peace-maker.

This little story emphasises the importance of compromise; of emphasising the positive rather than the negative; and above all the effort to put yourself in your partner's shoes, and looking at the whole issue from his/her point of view. Unfortunately, when a quarrel arises, couples just speak in anger – and respond with more anger. If you wish the 'black mood' to end quickly, both of you must learn to control yourself. When you exercise self-control, you're cutting off fuel to the fire, which is sure to die quickly.

One has to realise that nobody is perfect. We all have our share of unpleasant quirks, foibles and eccentricities. An important part of marriage is to understand and make allowances for the failings of your partner. Every marriage will have its share of misunderstandings and differences. But the wise learn from them. You will find that you grow in emotional strength, wisdom and maturity. As one philosopher has said, "Adversity not only draws people together, but brings forth that beautiful inward friendship, just as the cold winter forms ice figures on window panes, which the warmth of the sun may efface."

Dr. Normal Vincent Peale has the following suggestions on 'conducting' a quarrel in marriage:

1) See to it that your disagreement proceeds in slow motion. If you 'let off steam' in the heat of the moment, you will live to regret it.

2) In an emotionally charged crisis, don't hit back or counterpunch. Allow your spouse to finish what he/she wishes to say. Remember, speech is silver, silence is golden.

3) Remember to emphasise the positive. Be aware of the ideal of give and take. Look at the problem from your partner's point of view.

4) Become sensitive to the moods of your partner. This will tell you when to be gentle and patient, and when to be tough.

5) It is always a good thing to communicate your expectations and disappointments. Speaking out is far better than brooding on such matters. But even as you confess your dissatisfaction, look at each other's weaknesses and failings as opportunities for strengthening your bonds. Learn to give and take support, encouragement and understanding.

6) God designed men and women with divine wisdom to complement each other. Take a fresh look at yourselves from this perspective.

7) Work constantly to be in tune with each other, to understand each other, anticipate the other's needs, and to blend your lives together in harmony.

A lady I know was visiting a gastro-entrologist for a check-up. The doctor suspected that the patient may be prone to ulcer. "What kind of food do you eat ma'am?" he asked her casually.

"Oh doctor, I never ever eat spicy or oily food. In fact, we don't ever fry anything in my kitchen!"

Perhaps the lady expected to be praised for her austerity. All that the doctor said was, "How dreadful! I wouldn't want to be your guest!"

So it is with 'perfect' marriages in which the partners claim that they have never been angry with each other, or uttered a harsh word in anger. It would be a very dull and boring marriage indeed!

This is not to suggest that bitter quarrels are healthy and good for marriage. Constant quarrelling can damage any relationship. But if the disagreement is constructive and handled in the right way, it can actually strengthen the marriage.

Second Commandment of Marriage: Be a Good Listener

Listen to what the other person has to say. We like to talk but are not prepared to listen. Let us be good listeners. Of a couple it was said, "There was a time when he talked and she listened. On their honeymoon, she talked and he listened. Now that they are settled down in their own home, both talk and the neighbours listen."

It was Benjamin Disraeli who said, "Nature endowed man with two ears and one mouth. Man is meant to talk less and listen more." If man was meant to talk more and listen less he would have two mouths on the two sides of the face and one ear in front. How funny we would have looked! And the ears are made like funnels: they have no doors with which they can be closed. Whereas, if a word has to leave the mouth, it has to cross two fences – the fence of the two rows of teeth and the fence of the two lips.

Therefore, before a word is spoken we must at least think twice.

Of the spoken word we are slaves: of the unspoken word we are masters. Once a word leaves the lips, it cannot be taken back. Therefore, we must be careful of every word we speak. We should speak less, listen more. And we should listen not merely with the ears but with the heart. Better than talking is listening. Better than both is to enter the silence within. A saint of South India, Avvayar prayed, "O Lord, I keep on talking and talking as though I have mouths all over the body. When shall I cease from doing so? When shall I enter into the silence within?"

Someone said to me the other day, "It is hard to come by a good listener these days." You cannot get people to listen to you. Everyone is so wrapped up with their own concerns that they don't have time or patience to devote to anything/anyone else. But if you want to build a happy home and family you must learn to be a good listener. You must let your partner speak. You must hear him/her out patiently.

At meetings, discussions and even in get-togethers I hear people say again and again, "But let me finish..." "Let me finish, please!" Someone is trying to make a point, but he is interrupted so often that he cannot finish what he wants to say.

I am told that on an average a human being speaks thirty thousand words every day. This works out to over two hundred thousand words every week – over *ten million* words every year! If you are over fifty years old, you have already spoken 500 million words – but to what avail? How many of those words were really useful? How many of them were merely idle? For all those millions of idle words, you will have to render an account. Therefore, as a very wholesome principle of life, learn to ask yourself, "Are the words I am going to utter now, better than silence?" As it is said, *speech is silvern, silence is golden*. Therefore speak only when necessary. Speak only that which is good, pleasant, true and not hurtful to others.

Very often, one partner in a marriage has legitimate grievances, but the other is complaining too loudly to listen. Marriage can thrive only on a two-way communication!

"She's always talking and I do nothing but listen," some husbands claim. I would like to tell them that they must distinguish between *hearing, listening* and *effective listening*.

Counsellors tell us that hearing involves collecting sound-waves with your ears and processing them in your brain.

Listening involves both hearing and *paying attention*. Let us say for example that the news is on TV, and your spouse is talking to you at the same time. You may absorb the sound waves from both sources, but you can concentrate only on one! If, like some people, you are annoyed by the interruption, you may become upset and distracted and fail to listen to either.

Effective listening involves much more than hearing and listening. You observe carefully, interpret your partner's mood, action and body language, clarify and confirm the message you receive and then respond with sympathy and understanding.

Effective listening is of critical importance in marriage. It has even been said that listening is your window into your spouse's world. It is an opportunity for you to make your spouse realise that his/her concerns are important to you. In order to achieve this you must:

- Let your partner be aware that you are listening. You must not keep watching TV or reading a newspaper. You must not yawn, look at your watch or fidget in your seat. One way of ensuring that your partner knows that you are listening is to keep continuous eye-contact. This is sure to encourage better communication.

- Verbally acknowledge what your partner is telling you: this can be done with the help of simple phrases like, "Go on, I am listening," or "I understand what you are saying," or "Tell me more," or other similar expressions. A well-chosen phrase like, "I know what you mean honey," can make a world of difference, and will ensure that your partner understands your emotional receptivity.

- Try not to interrupt your partner midway: even if your impulse is to defend yourself or counter a point, exercise restraint so that your partner may finish what he/she is trying to say.

- Ask for clarifications; communicate to your partner that you have understood her/his point of view. When you summarise or restate what you have heard, it assures your partner that you have listened carefully, and that you have not misunderstood whatever was said. Do not make any assumptions on your own.

You will forgive me if I return to the basics once again: all communication requires two basic necessities – a speaking voice and a listening ear. Alas, these are taken for granted but they are hardly available! Most of us practise selective listening, switching off and switching on as it suits us.

There is external noise all around us; there is internal distraction which makes it worse! Surely, it is tragic when we are not in tune with – or even tune out – those whom we love!

I am told that there are several wives of the older generation who have been unable to communicate meaningfully with their husbands. They may ask questions like, "What should I cook today?" and get appropriate answers– but that is hardly what I would call meaningful communication. Whenever these women have something important to convey to their husbands, they call upon their children – grown up sons or daughters – to talk to their father.

Thus it is that we begin to turn what is called "a deaf ear" to our spouses.

Misunderstandings due to poor listening have caused a lot of misery in many marriages. When you fail to listen to your spouse, you cause pain and unhappiness – this leads to loneliness, alienation, hurt, and wasted moments of precious life.

In Voltaire's story *Candide*, the hero and heroine dream and plan their future lives together. Unfortunately, both of them are too self-centered to listen to the other's ideas. Her dreams are all about material wealth – rubies, pearls, marble palaces with extensive gardens and swimming pools. His dreams are idyllic – to live simply on a few acres of land, with a pig, a cow and a kitchen garden to potter about in. Naturally, disaster and disillusion ensue for the couple.

A little boy who had just started school, complained that he had been sent to the wrong school. "I can't read or write," he said mournfully, "and they won't let me talk! What can I do?"

Of course, the joke books are full of the 'other side' of the story. Have you heard about the two boys who were bragging about the abilities of their mothers? "My Mom can talk for an hour on any subject you give her," said one. "That's nothing," scoffed the other. "My Mama can talk for one hour *without* any subject. Ask my Daddy!"

"Stop, look and listen! That is the story of every man's life," said a young husband.

"What do you mean?" his friend enquired.

"You see a pretty girl, you stop; you look; after you marry her, for the rest of your life you listen!"

The doctor said to the patient's wife, "Your husband needs complete rest and quiet. I am going to prescribe these sleeping pills."

"When should he have them, doctor?" enquired the wife anxiously.

"Oh no, they are not for him," said the doctor. "You can take them every night, so he can have peace and quiet!"

But jokes apart, I think it is ironic that with all the progress we have made in 'communication technology' as it is called, with the ability to talk to people in every corner of the globe at the touch of a button, we have failed to bridge the ever-widening gaps within our own families.

But there is hope. Listening is an art that we can all learn. Concern for the feelings and emotional well-being of your spouse will surely prompt you to change your listening habits, for you hear best when you love! But I urge you to —

1. Listen to your spouse carefully.

2. Listen to your spouse's full story.

3. Listen to your spouse's full story first – before you react.

Human relations are bound to remain superficial, if you do not learn to *listen* carefully to the other person. Unfortunately, many of us remain *deaf* and *blind* to others' feelings!

Let me tell you the familiar story of a man who was really physically deaf. He went to visit a friend in hospital.

The friend had been languishing in illness for a long time, and had reached the end of his tether. He was praying to the Lord to relieve him of the burden of life.

The deaf man asked his friend, "How are you doing, my dear fellow?" (He had planned the entire conversation carefully earlier. He did not want his deafness to hamper his meeting with his friend. Now he imagined that his friend would say, "I'm much better now, thank you!")

104

In reality, the embittered patient said, "I'm just waiting to die."

"That's good!" exclaimed the deaf man, and you can imagine how the conversation proceeded.

"Are they looking after you well here in this hospital?"

"They are all *yama dootas* (messengers of the god of death) here," was the reply.

"Thank God, I'm so pleased to hear it. What do you eat these days?"

"Poison!"

"Good! I hope your digestion is good."

You may laugh at this absurd conversation. But in reality, we are little better than the deaf man, when we fail to listen sensitively to our partners.

Being too wrapped up in their own concerns and interests, people do not attempt to understand others. They are quite *deaf* to others' needs. This can lead to serious disharmony in married life. When disharmony creeps in, words and actions are misunderstood. Hurts and wounds are inflicted. All because people cannot or will not listen to one another!

Third Command Of Marriage: Appreciate Your Spouse

Everyone loves to be appreciated. Do not find fault with your spouse when you are in the midst of other people. Leonardo da Vinci said: "Reprove your friend in secret, praise him before others." When we appreciate others, we help them to draw out the best that is in them. Appreciate others.

Appreciate your children. Do not scold them. When you scold your children, you stifle the life force that is within them. I asked a child what his name was. And he answered, "In school, they call me Ramesh, at home I am called Ramesh don't." I could not understand. And he explained, "At school they call me Ramesh. But at home they tell me, Ramesh don't do this. Ramesh don't behave like this. Ramesh don't talk like this. Ramesh don't sit like this. At home

I am Ramesh don't." Today, as you return to your homes, go and appreciate your spouses. May I pass on to you a magic formula? It is built up of seven simple words. It can create a new atmosphere in the home. The seven words are *"Honey, where would I be without you?"* Those words must be spoken atleast once every day, not mechanically but with deep feeling and emotion of the heart. "Honey where would I be without you?"

The most ardent and happy marriage may become dull and colourless if the couple begin to take each other for granted. A feeling of complacency descends on the relationship, and the marriage tends to become jaded and listless. Something is felt to be missing! Appreciate your spouse and that will put the sparkle back into your marriage. Joseph Choate, a diplomat, was once asked what he would like to be if he had the opportunity to be born again. He replied without a moment's hesitation, "I would like to be Mrs. Choate's husband again!"

In India too, conservative Hindu wives utter a traditional prayer in which they express the desire to be married to their husband in all the lives to come; what a beautiful thought this is!

All of us are yearning to be appreciated. All of us love to receive compliments, which assure us that we are loved and appreciated. Mark Twain once remarked that he could go on for about two months without a good compliment – but no longer.

When you express your appreciation of your spouse, you give recognition to her strengths, or prop her up where she needs most support. You do not have to be insincere or resort to flattery. An honest compliment is simple and uttered from the heart; it costs nothing to give, but its worth is truly inestimable!

Actually, it is not very difficult to offer an honest compliment: each of us has many positive qualities. When you take the trouble to identify these 'positives' in your spouse and compliment her on it, you will not only make her happy, but you will build up her self-esteem.

In addition to this, I urge couples to go through a session of sharing the good things in their life, whenever they can. This simply means paying each other compliments and expressing appreciation of the blessings conferred upon them through marriage.

There was a man whose greatest ambition was to own a house with a small garden. "I'd love to live in an independent house," he would tell his wife over and over again.

As it happened, the couple had to settle for an apartment. The husband was obviously disappointed, for his dream had never left him.

However, the wife was a sensitive and sympathetic soul. Everyday she would find something to praise about the flat – its location, the neighbours, the view from the balcony, the well-planned kitchen, etc. "Aren't we lucky to be here!" she would say. "I'm so glad you bought this place for us."

Need I tell you that in time, the husband too grew to love the flat. And in his heart of hearts, he was deeply grateful for his wife's appreciation which turned a disappointment into an achievement.

All it takes is a little sympathy, understanding, kindness and a flair for the right words – and you can express your appreciation in style!

A middle-aged couple were attending a party. The wife was persuaded to sing a song – she sang so well that the guests gave her a standing ovation. Taken aback by the response to his wife's song, the husband blurted out, " I did not know that she could sing so well!"

Do you really know your partner well? Do you take the trouble to find out her likes and dislikes? Or are you one of those people who have no time or interest in such things? Do you remember birthdays and anniversaries? How often do you say to your partner, "Honey, where would I be without you?"

If your spouse has a special talent or gift, encourage her, appreciate her. Participate in her interests; allow her to grow.

I know a man who married a young girl fresh out of college. On their honeymoon, he asked her what she liked best.

"I love studying," said the young lady spontaneously. "I was always top of my class you know!" Quietly, she added, "My ambition was to do a Ph.D.!"

"And so you shall!" her young husband promised. He was as good as his word. He helped her pursue post-graduate studies. He took her to libraries. He bought books for her. He freed her from all household chores when her exams came up. He filled up forms and stood in the queue to pay her fees. He encouraged her and motivated her to do her best until she obtained the coveted doctoral degree. The lady is now a happy mother of two children and a research scientist who is highly respected in her chosen field. What she achieved was possible because of loving appreciation!

If your wife enjoys playing the *sitar* or the *veena* or the piano, encourage her to pursue her interest. This way, you participate meaningfully in her interest; you allow her to be herself and to evolve. Above all, you appreciate her skills and share what is important to her. If she enjoys going to the *satsang*, you should join her in going to the *satsang*.

If your husband enjoys long and leisurely walks, join him for a stroll. Give up your TV or your newspaper and rearrange your routine so that you can be together in an activity he enjoys.

Couples should learn to share and appreciate each other's tastes. Do not criticise your husband's choice of colour. Do not tell your wife that the neighbour's cooking is better.

I am afraid husbands are often to blame in this – they become so excessively involved in their work and business that they take their wives for granted. They stay back late in their offices, while their wives wait interminably for them to come home. This leads to feelings of neglect, frustration and loneliness. When the husband does come home, he eats dinner in silence and then flops in front of the TV. He is too tired to talk, he tells his wife. She ends up feeling as if she were a piece of furniture.

Consider how the whole scenario would change if the husband, on entering, asks his wife, "How was your day, honey? Tell me about it!"

Nowadays both partners work outside the home. Both are pursuing careers and living hectic, professional lives. It is even more important that they should take time out to talk to each other, share their feelings and express their appreciation for each other. This sense of understanding and appreciation should grow with time, so that the bonds of marriage are nourished and strengthened.

Learn to appreciate your spouse! Your wife prepares delicacies and dainty dishes to tickle your palate – and waits for a word of approval, a hint or gesture of appreciation. "Mmm! That was delicious!"

would delight her. "That's a new recipe, isn't it? I liked it," would please her indeed!

A young lady once said to me that when she tried very hard to present a special dish, her husband would murmer, "For a change, the food is good today," or, "How come I am not getting dog food today?"

I hope many of you can do better than that at your compliments! But alas, many men imitate the sphinx at dinner table. They remain inscrutably silent, and make sure not a word of appreciation escapes their lips!

Let me repeat the magic formula. It consists of just seven words – and it can bring about a miraculous transformation in your life. The seven words are: "Honey, where would I be without you?"

"Honey, where would I be without you?" I offered this magic formula for the first time when I was in Hong Kong, several years ago. I was delivering a public lecture there, and the meeting was presided over by a man of eighty years.

I met him again the next day, when he came to attend another of my lectures. He was not the president of the evening, but he came up to ask me whether he could speak a few words before I started.

I agreed and he came up to the podium and said, "I would like to tell you all that last evening, I put into practice a valuable suggestion offered by Dada. I went home and whispered to my wife, *'Honey, where would I be without you?'* I tell you, my wife was dazed. She could not grasp the meaning of those words! So I said it again, *'Honey, where would I be without you?'*

"When the meaning of the words dawned on her, she gave me such an ecstatic hug as she has not given me in 55 years of married life! I urge you all, to take up this magic formula!"

Appreciate your spouse! You will create a new atmosphere, a new world in your home!

A little girl I met once told me, "My mother cannot bake cakes or make ice-cream at home. But she makes the best *dal* in the world!"

Children can be very appreciative and loyal. It was not a problem for the child that her mother could not cook fancy dishes. In her generosity, she declared her mother to be the best *dal*–maker in the world!

Another mother told me, that she was thrilled when she got little notes of appreciation from her husband. It could be for a special meal, a kind word she had said, or just patient listening that she gave to him. "I'm so glad I have you," the note would say. Or, " I'm so proud of you," or even, " How hard you work for me!"

One day, a husband returned home from work, weary and stressed. As he entered the home, the wife took his briefcase from him and said, lovingly, "Would you like a cold drink first or will you have dinner right away? You look exhausted darling!"

The husband was overcome. What had he done to deserve this – that a loving, caring woman should be waiting at home to receive him with a smile, offering food, drink and whatever he needed?

He blurted his thoughts out to her in so many words – and how her face lit up!

That is the magic of appreciation.

Fourth Commandment Of Marriage: Keep Your Love Fresh!

After marriage, spouses take each other for granted. Women have complained to me, "There was a time when our husbands gave us many promises, made many vows, took great interest in what we did. All that has become a part of history. Now they take us for granted." Therefore, keep your love fresh.

It was a wise woman who remarked, "Of course my husband and I take each other's love for granted! We are sure and secure about our love. But we never take each other for granted!"

It is not enough for husbands to earn money to support the family. It is not enough for wives to cook and clean and launder. Marriage involves much more than such material needs. Listen to the emotional needs of your partners. Absorb the spirit of their conversation. Appreciate their dreams and aspirations. Learn to support and encourage them in every way.

I always think that it is good to develop a healthy sense of 'dependence' on your spouse. I am quite sceptical about 'open' and 'free' marriages where husbands and wives give each other the 'freedom' to do as they please. Long-distance marriages which are becoming common nowadays alarm me.

Emotional and physical independence come easily to men and women these days. I think there is something valuable about a relationship where husband and wife need each other, and are vulnerable without the other's support.

Consider a couple who are leading "full, active lives" as they put it. The husband is a busy executive; he jet-sets all over the world; he attends seminars, conferences and business meetings every other day; he entertains customers, foreign collaborators and visiting consultants to lunch or dinner at five-star hotels; and at weekends, he relaxes by playing golf with select friends....

As for the wife, she is 'into' yoga and fitness; she visits fashion designers; she is a regular member of the Ladies' club where she plays cards with her friends every day; she is also learning to design jewellery and hopes to open her own outlet soon...

They are beginning to go in separate revolving circles. They are in danger of becoming married strangers. They live under the same roof, eat at the same table and share a bed every night... but they are drifting apart.

They must learn to be flexible. Each should be willing to change, give in just a little for the sake of the marriage. They should spare more time to be in each other's company. They should spend more time with the children. They should 'loosen' their schedules and deadlines so that their marriage does not suffer. They should work for change. They should work to keep their love fresh!

Nobody wants to live an emotionally barren existence! No one likes to live in a separate revolving circle!

A highly respected marriage counsellor tells people, "Take the trouble to *study* your partner. Make an effort to understand him/her. Consider him/her as a rare and fascinating object. Study him constantly. Understand his likes and dislikes. Appreciate her strengths and weaknesses. Be sensitive to his moods and feelings. If you wish to live successfully with your marriage partner, you must get to know the person better each and every day. You must learn to know what pleases him; you must know what upsets her; you must know when to encourage him and when not to push him too hard. In other words, do not ever take your partner for granted.

Many men take quick decisions – and having once made up their minds, stick to their guns. Women, on the other hand, have a tough time taking decisions. There are so many issues and considerations which sway them. This calls for a major adjustment – but it can be accomplished with love and patience.

There was a lady who needed to travel to the US to be with her daughter who was about to give birth to her first child. It was decided that she would travel in February, for the confinement was expected in March. The husband would fly out to join them in April, after the baby was born.

Accordingly, the flight reservations were made. The mother was to fly out on Feb 1st. On 28th January, she developed mild blood pressure. The doctor assured them that it was nothing but stress, and that there was nothing to stop her from flying, as scheduled.

"I think I'll fly a little later," she said to her husband. He readily agreed. The flight was changed to 5th February, and the daughter was informed.

On 3rd February, the lady was afflicted with a severe allergy. "I'll leave on the 10th", she pleaded with her husband. And he agreed.

On 8th February, she began to suffer from acidity. When the father called his daughter in the US, she said to him, "Papa, I suggest you fly in with Mama. I think she doesn't want to travel alone without you."

The husband was a kind and loving man. He said to his wife, "Honey, there's no need for you to feel so tense. We shall fly together to be with our daughter. Does that make you feel better?"

The wife cheered up instantly. Her numerous afflictions disappeared miraculously. In gratitude and appreciation, she held her husband's hand and said to him, "Thank you! The truth is that I did not want to leave you and go alone!"

Eventually, the daughter sent them fresh reservations to fly together to the US on Feb 14th –

St. Valentine's Day! They knew how to keep their love fresh!

Take a good look at some of the following expressions:

"I am proud of you!"

"You make me feel good!"

"I love to be seen with you."

"My self-confidence gets a boost when you are with me."

"You have the ability to make me feel great!"

"Your sense of humour is terrific. I love it when you make me laugh!"

"I am so glad you are watching over me. I don't make mistakes when you are around!"

"Thank you for being you!"

And of course the seven-word magic formula, *"Honey, were would I be without you?"*

In everyone of the above expressions is the underlying message – I love you! You make me feel happy and secure.

This is the secret of keeping married love fresh – permanently!

Fifth Commandment Of Marriage: Do Not Expect Perfection Of Each Other

No man or woman is ever perfect. It was Jesus who said: "Call me not perfect. Alone the Father in Heaven is Perfect!" Marriage involves the coming together of two imperfect human beings. Accept your spouse for what he or she is, not for what he or she would be, could be, or should be.

In a Christian marriage ceremony, the couple vows to be by each other, love each other and cherish each other, "till death do us part." Through rain and sunshine, sorrow and joy, laughter and tears, they promise to be together.

In a Hindu marriage, the following blessing is pronounced on the newly weds:

> This union shall stay unchanged through the different stages of life. (i.e., during periods of

122

happiness and unhappiness.) Old age does not take away the inter-dependence of the souls. Passing through the sweet and bitter experiences of life, you will emerge steadier and stronger in love. Only the lucky ones are blessed with such a rare union.

How may you achieve such a rare and blessed union? The answer is simple; through selfless love. Selfless love seeks to understand, accept, sympathise, forgive and appreciate. Selfish love, on the other hand, makes demands and nourishes impossible expectations.

I am afraid young people today expect too much from married life. They look for material comfort, complete fulfilment and a sense of achievement. Young girls dream of the perfect man – handsome, kind, highly qualified, wealthy, and intelligent. As for young men – they dream of tall, slim, fair princesses who look like film stars but can cook like their grandmothers. Such people suffer from painful disillusion, when they find that the reality of life cannot match up to their fantasies. They suffer from disappointment and frustration; they feel cheated, they think they have made a ghastly mistake.

They *have* made a mistake, but that mistake was to expect too much from marriage in the first place.

The truth is, happy marriages are based on the principle of give and take. One of the fundamental requirements of a successful marriage is to accept your partner with love and understanding – to learn to live and love selflessly.

Marriages are not meant to be magical tricks. Peace and contentment and happiness of the heart are not handed to you on a platter as a wedding present from God. You have to work to earn them.

It is good for young men and women to go in with a clear eyed realisation that life has its limitations, and marriages have their store of problems. When you adopt a realistic and compassionate approach to life and people, you will grow in understanding and maturity and your marriage can become truly rewarding.

I know some people who pride themselves on being 'perfectionists'. I appreciate them as long as they aim for perfection in all that *they* say and do. But when they begin to demand perfection (as per *their* standards) from their partners, they are only asking for trouble!

I am told that in the olden days, irate husbands would fling their plates (filled with food) away, if the salt content was not right or if any item on the menu was less than perfect.

They thought that this would ensure 'perfection' in their wives. Isn't it horrifying to contemplate?

It has been said that if we look *for* love we will never find it; we should always look *with* love.

Have you heard of the old saying, "A watched kettle never boils". When we are constantly looking for something to happen, the very act of constant expectation seems to delay the awaited event! So too in marriage, when you keep an eagerly expectant eye on the partner, you are doomed to disappointment. I would urge you to train those eagle eyes on yourself instead and try hard to become the perfect partner yourself!

When you adopt a critical judgemental attitude, there is the danger of the relationship being stunted and suffocated. Love cannot flourish under the critical gaze!

The ideal "look of love" should possess insight, the ability to look within and enable you to look at your partner with tolerance, understanding, forgiveness and optimism.

125

Psychologist Carl Jung writes, "If things go wrong...I shall put myself right first."

As human beings, none of us is perfect. Frailties and imperfections abound in each of us. We succumb to anger, falsehood, prejudice, and hate so easily and so often. When we learn to love each other in spite of these failings we truly *rise* in love, instead of *falling out* of love!

Henry Ford was once asked, "Who is your best friend?" His reply is significant: " Your best friend is the person who brings out of you the best that is in you."

If you are married, become the best friend of your spouse! Look for the vein of gold hidden within your partner and do everything you can to expose that gold! You will find that you yourself will evolve and mature in the process, and you will learn to encourage, compliment and support your partner in every way.

This story was narrated to me by a man who became a widower and subsequently married a second time. His first marriage had been a disaster. His wife continuously nagged him and criticised his every word and gesture. "I'd like you to conform to my high standards," she would say. "I want to make you perfect in every way."

And she interfered in everything – "This is not what you should wear," "This is how you should talk," "You should not do this," "You must not go there," etc. etc. She insisted that every aspect of his life should be honed to near perfection.

Unable to cope with these excessive demands, the man said to her one day, "I can't take your criticism any more. I know you mean well. So why don't you just write down all that you expect me to do?"

She promptly complied. But, as fate would have it, before she could complete the list or he could begin to read it, she passed away. The list lay, forgotten, in his desk.

A few years later, the man married again – but not without considerable trepidation. After all, he had not exactly managed to please his first wife; how far would he succeed with the second?

To his surprise and relief, his new marriage was a great success. He could hardly believe the joy and peace and security he felt in the home. He himself became far more self-confident and good humoured.

One day, several years later, he came across the list of 'do's and don'ts' compiled by his first wife. He read them for the first time, and was amazed to realise that he was actually following all of them now – even though his second wife had never ever mentioned them.

He thought for a while and realised the difference. His first wife had always begun by saying, " I hate it when ...." His new wife always started off by saying, " I love it when ...."

Do not expect or demand perfection of your spouse. Even a word, a gesture, a wrong tone of voice can cause friction in marriage. Therefore, speak gently.

Sixth Commandment Of Marriage : Be A Good Forgiver

To make marriage a success, to make it a source of happiness and harmony, you have to forgive much. It is the prerogative of marriage to give and give and give – and forgive – and never be tired of giving and forgiving. "How many times shall I forgive?" asked a husband. "Shall I forgive 7 times?" "No," came the answer, "you must forgive 70 times 7!" 70 times 7 is 490 times which means you must forgive without counting. And a wife complained, "I have been forgiving until I can forgive no longer. I have forgiven and received nothing in return." And she was told: "Continue to forgive without expecting anything in return."

Forgiveness is the characteristic trait of selfless, unconditional love. It has rightly been described as the 'emotional disarmament' in marriage.

Forgiveness in marriage is not based on 'logic' or 'justice'. I once heard a woman exclaim to her husband, "I am not logical. I am not predictable. You can't programme me. I am a human being!"

Forgiveness is not logical or methodical. It must be spontaneous. It is simple and straightforward – you accept your spouse's shortcomings and you continue to love. When you forgive your spouse, you both feel better! Thus forgiveness is its own reward!

As I have said repeatedly, no human being is perfect. Therefore, no marriage is perfect either. Misunderstandings, accidents and quarrels will inevitably occur in any relationship. These may be over in a flash, but then, bitter memories linger.

Some of us forgive easily; but cannot forget. And this is not enough. Therefore I urge you to erase the bitter memories of the past so that your happy future may not be clouded. An honest apology, a generous acknowledgement and loving forgiveness – that's all it takes to wipe out the bitterness and anger. When this is done with all sincerity and good faith, you can make a fresh beginning and pursue the possibility of "living happily ever after" as the story books describe it.

There is a story of a Russian couple who were deeply in love with each other. Though they had been married for several years, they kept their love fresh. They made a pact with each other that, every morning, the husband would wake up before the wife and prepare tea. He would bring a cup of tea to his wife and whisper in her ear, "Honey, here is tea for you!" The wife would wake up with a loving look in her grateful eyes.

You, too, must keep your love fresh. Life, without an element of romance, is dry as the desert-sands. The common complaint of many women is that their husbands take them for granted, they pay them scant attention. This should not be so. Tonight, as you return to your home, go and whisper into the ear of your wife, "Honey, you mean so much to me!" you will be rewarded with a rich and grateful glow in her eyes. New joy will wake up in her heart. It is such a simple thing. Just try it!

Of a great English poet I read that he never spoke a word of appreciation to his wife. So long as she lived, he criticised her, found fault with many things she did. Suddenly, the wife died. The poet exclaimed, "Ah, if only you had given me some notice, I would have written poem after poem in your praise, and expressed my heart's gratitude for all that you did for me!"

We recognise the worth of a person only when he is dead. We place wreaths on his dead body and pay glowing tributes to him at memorial meetings. Let us do something for our dear ones, while they are still alive.

Tonight, as you return to your homes, fling a surprise on your wife and let her know how much you love her.

The famous magician, Houdini, kept his love fresh till the very end. He found time, everyday, to write a love-letter to his wife. From 1913, till his death, whether he was in or out of town, he did not let a day pass without writing some words of affection to her.

Keep your love fresh, but do not be attached to anyone. Attachment is the root of sorrow. No one belongs to you: you belong to the Lord. Therein lies the secret of the art of living. Alone you came into this world: alone, you will leave it. In the mid-period, give as much love as you can to those that cross the pathways of your life. Give love to all, and forgive the wrongs done to you. Give love to all, seeking no revenge for offences and insults.

The great Italian Poet, Tasso, was asked why he did not take revenge upon a man who had hurt him greatly. The Poet answered, "I do not desire to plunder him, yet there is one thing I would like to take from him."

"His honour, his wealth, his life?" Tasso asked.

"No," came the gentle reply. "What I desire to take from him, I will try to gain by the exercise of kindness, patience and forbearance. I will try to take away his ill-will." That is the way to burn anger before anger burns us.

The Russian couple kept their love fresh. Every evening, as the husband returned from the office, his wife would wait for him at the gate and welcome him. They would hug each other, enter the house and speak of all that had transpired during the day.

One day, for no fault of the husband, his boss lost his temper and was mad at him for some work which had not been done properly. The husband's feelings were hurt. When he returned home, in the evening, he saw his wife waiting at the gate, but paid her no attention. As he walked into the house, the wife asked,

"Honey, what is the matter? Has something gone wrong? Tell me, if only to take the burden off your mind!"

The irate husband blurted out, "Why must you keep on chattering all the time? Why don't you shut up? I do not want to hear your silly voice anymore."

The wife was stunned. The lotus of her heart drooped and she resolved never to speak to her husband again. "He does not want to hear my silly voice! I shall not let him hear it."

This went on for forty years. The husband, of course, repented. Repeatedly, he begged for forgiveness. But the wound created in the heart of the wife by those sharp, angry words was too deep. She could never make up her mind to speak to her husband. He was now on his death-bed. He pleaded with her, "Pray, speak just one word of forgiveness to me, so that I may die in peace." She felt helpless. Words just would not come out of her lips.

Let me tell you friends, nothing is gained from harbouring an unforgiving, unforgetting attitude in our hearts. "You forgot my birthday last year," or "You did not let me take that golfing weekend with my friends," or, "You made me do this or that...."

Forgiveness is not only extended to your spouse – it requires a healing process *inside* you so that you do not feel any bitterness or resentment about what happened. As I have said repeatedly, "I can forgive, but I cannot forget," is only another way of saying, "I will *not* forgive."

Seventh Commandment Of Marriage: You Must Be Patient, Loving, Understanding, Kind and True To Each Other

I am afraid many of us have a rather shallow and superficial conception of love and marriage. We look upon love as something romantic – a thing of the heart. We regard it as something intangible, ephemeral, something which we can't even find words to describe.

Native American Indians look upon love as a kind of wisdom. They believe that love is the first wisdom given to us, and we derive all else from that knowledge.

When I hear people talk of 'love-at-first-sight', I express the silent wish that this may include *insight* and *foresight* as well as *hindsight!* "Love happened in a flash!" young lovers often claim. If you don't want it to be just a flash-in-a-pan, you must grow in understanding and knowledge of each other.

I met a man who was walking to school with his daughter. He greeted me enthusiastically, and I enquired after the sweet little child who held his hands and looked at me with polite interest.

"Oh, this is my third child Vinita, she's studying in the third standard!" he said.

The child's face fell. "Oh Papa," she protested. "I'm in the fourth! Anita is in the third!"

It might have been a matter of indifference to the man as to which class the child was in, but it mattered to her that her Papa knew exactly what she was doing!

If love is to grow and endure, it must be constantly nourished by understanding, shared experiences, sympathy, patience and compassion. Such love is powerful – it has the power to heal, unite, enrich and restore. This is why a great European thinker said, "Love is the driving force for the highest values of human life: to the power of truth, knowledge, beauty, freedom, goodness and happiness."

"What is the best way to understand?" someone asked me. I could only reply, "The best way to understand is to be understanding."

Did you know that the word understand is actually related to its literal meaning – i.e., stand under something? You have to observe something from the bottom to the top.

Unfortunately, we are losing the ability to understand others. We rush into snap judgements. We develop strong opinions on everything and everyone – even when we really don't know about them.

Understanding helps you to grow in the spirit of humility. To understand is to stand under! Unfortunately, no one is prepared to stand under anyone else today. Everyone wants to stand above everyone else – no wonder then, that the divorce rate is increasing, and our homes are breaking! Parents say they cannot understand their children; children claim they cannot understand their parents.

"Why should I stay at home and look after the children?" young women argue. "Let our husbands do the cooking and the cleaning too!"

"Why should I help with the house work and the children?" husbands want to know. "I bring in the money and I will not lift a finger in my own home!"

Humility and understanding are the keys to harmony and happiness. When you learn to love and respect your spouse, when you begin to appreciate his/her special qualities, then your marriage bonds are strengthened.

I am often disappointed and grieved when married men or women use the word "my" instead of "our". How often do people not say, "my car", "my house", "my son", "my daughter", "my bank account" etc. What is the purpose of marriage if you can't begin to substitute *us* for *me, ours* for *mine?*

We must work constantly to remove egotism and materialism from love. "If you really love me, you must buy me a diamond ring for my birthday," a wife demands of her husband. "If you really love me, don't contradict anything I say," a husband tells his wife. This is a very narrow selfish notion of love. Such people are not interested in equal partners: they only want someone who will constantly glorify them, pamper them, flatter them and reinforce their ego. When their partners disagree, or offer a differing opinion, this is regarded as 'unloving' behaviour.

I would call for a little more empathy among marriage partners. Empathy is nothing but understanding the other person's point of view. The golden command do-as-you-would-be-done-by is a splendid instance of empathy. It is an excellent technique for strengthening marriage bonds.

Do you consider yourself to be sensitive, vulnerable and very, very special? Think of your spouse too, in the same way. Do you feel that you should never be hurt or upset or let down or disappointed by your partner? Extend the same courtesy to him/her. For empathy is based on mutual respect. We will develop the spirit of empathy when we learn to step out of our rigid, inflexible positions and view the world from another's perspective.

Egocentric love demands that the other person should live, act and do everything for our benefit alone! I'm afraid that it is demeaning and degrading to regard a partner as someone who can be possessed and controlled. Absolute control over another person is inhuman and undesirable. As the wise saying goes, "The bird of paradise alights only upon the hand that does not grasp."

Tolerance is a great virtue in this age of individuality and self-assertion. Tolerance is nothing but the sincere effort to understand, appreciate and respect your partner's beliefs and habits. This does not mean you simply accept the other's point of view. It only means that you make an effort to understand it!

"I know how to keep my wife in her place," remarked a boastful husband. "I know exactly how to put her down." "He had better not try to contradict me in any way," observed a haughty wife. "One word from me – and he knows who wins the game"

I think that is the most destructive and demeaning way to tackle differences in marriage. True love enhances; it does not degrade or devalue. True love builds up the spouse's self-respect and does not diminish it in any way. If you truly love someone how can you belittle that person?

There was a husband who constantly put his wife down in the presence of friends, guests and even strangers. "Oh she's practically illiterate," he would sneer. "Fifth-standard-failed." Or "She is really clumsy, my wife," and so on and so on.

One day at a party, he uttered one of his snide remarks, "She can never get anything straight, ever!" She turned round and said to him, loud and clear, so

141

that everyone heard her, "Honey, if I am so awful and worthless, why did you marry me in the first place?"

The husband was rendered speechless, for he had no answer to that question.

Insults and caustic comments will never change anyone for the better. They will only aggravate the situation. When there are so many ways to persuade and influence your partner in a positive sense, why should you resort to destructive methods like wounding words and degrading suggestions?

Many people suffer from a needless compulsion to change their partners. Wives want to change their husband's friends, his ties, his jackets and even his favourite music. Husbands want their wives to talk more (or less), laugh (more or less), grow slimmer or fairer, cut their hair or grow it.

What a sad thing it is when we can only find fault with people whom we love! We rarely realise that our complaints stem from our own peculiar whims and moods.

"People have one thing in common," says Robert Zend, "They are all different."

There was a woman who started to 'work on' her husband, determined to change him to suit her own preferences. She nagged, cajoled, begged, threatened; she moulded, shaped and influenced. After several years, she 'got him into shape' as she wanted. He was exactly what she had wanted him to be. But now she had a new problem. "He's just not the man I married," she sighed in frustration.

A happy and healthy relationship requires that you should give each other the space and time you both need to be on your own. It is both possible and desirable that within the framework of marriage, the partners should be able to maintain their individuality and creativity. This does not just mean having large rooms for your exclusive use where you can paint or sing. After all, how many of us live in mansions? What I mean by space is really the freedom and the opportunity to pursue those interests which your spouse does not share.

For instances, a husband may set up a computer or some fitness equipment in the home, a wife may attend music lessons or a course in pottery and ceramics in the afternoon. This way, each of them

143

learns to live at peace with himself/herself and with the other.

Tina and Pravin are a devoted couple. Tina is energetic, fun-loving and a live-wire, taking interest in all that goes on around her. She is a member of the PTA in her son's school, and the cultural Secretary of their Housing Society. Weekly *bhajan* sessions and rehearsals for programmes keep her busy and occupied.

Pravin is a devout and pious man who calls himself a "practical businessman and an avid tennis-player." His mornings in the home are sacrosanct. He likes to perform a traditional *puja* that lasts an hour, and includes the recitation of different *mantras* each day of the week.

Tina and Pravin give each other the 'space' – the time and the freedom – to pursue those activities that matter to them. And they are proud of each other. "No committee can manage without Tina," says her husband proudly. "My husband balances his religion and his business beautifully," she says about him.

You don't have to shut yourself up or 'get rid' of your partner to give yourself space. You have to create space for yourself within your home and marriage.

The great secret of human happiness lies in understanding – and understanding, as we have seen, is indeed a complex art involving many things. It requires kindness and empathy; it involves tolerance and loving patience; it includes a healthy respect for the other's interests. As you make the effort to understand your spouse, you grow in the understanding of yourself and the events of life. You acquire wisdom and patience, and you learn to avoid those needless misunderstandings that waste so much time and energy.

Kamla and Kishore are a working couple. Kamla works in a bank and Kishore is a software engineer.

One day, Kamla was held up in the office due to the yearly closing of accounts. She requested her husband to do some shopping for her – buy some milk, bread and vegetables on his way home. "I'll make toasted sandwiches and coffee, and that will take care of the dinner," she said to him on the phone.

When Kamla entered the flat at 8:00 p.m. that night, Kishore was relaxing in front of the TV. "Hi, good to see you back so early!" he called out cheerfully. "I remember, last year your colleague brought you home at 10:00 p.m!"

Kamla was tired and hungry. Secretly, she was also irritated that Kishore was relaxing and watching TV at ease. She looked at the shopping bag on the sideboard and saw that it was empty. He had forgotten to do the shopping!

She was about to make some tea first and tell her husband all about her hectic day. She changed her mind and shut herself up in the bedroom, barely able to control her anger. He was so selfish and careless! Well, she would teach him a lesson. There was nothing to make dinner with, and he could settle for an enforced *upvas* (fasting).

She came out to get herself a drink of water from the fridge and found milk packets neatly laid out in the chiller. Oh good, she would make the tea after all. And when she turned on the gas stove she saw that bread had been neatly sliced and ready-prepared to be popped into the sandwich toaster. Kishore had sliced cucumbers, tomatoes and onions and lavishly spread cheese between the bread slices. Oh, how kind and sweet and loving her husband was! Kamla's eyes filled with tears of love and gratitude.

This is how misunderstanding can affect attitudes. When you misunderstand your spouse, you look at the situation with jaundiced eyes. When the truth dawns on you, you see things completely differently.

Understanding human nature is indeed a complex and challenging art. Each human being is unique – a profound and mysterious being.

Guru Arjun Dev tells us in the sacred *Sukhmani Sahib*: that *there is a lamb and a lion within each one of us*. Each rose has its share of thorns, amidst which the sublimely beautiful flower blooms. I think this symbolises the human predicament too.

"With all thy getting, get understanding," urges The Book of Proverbs. True! Understanding is the most precious quality a human being can possess. It cultivates your inner vision; it enhances the intuitive faculty which enables you to perceive the truth about yourself, others and your life.

Eighth Commandment Of Marriage: Develop A Healthy Sense Of Humour

If two people have to live with each other, they must develop a healthy sense of humour. They must learn to laugh and make each other laugh. We must laugh *with* others, never laugh *at* others. If we have to laugh at somebody, we must laugh at ourselves. Each one of us has some oddities, some unpleasant quirks or weaknesses. We can always laugh at ourselves. Laughter is at once a physical, mental and spiritual tonic.

A husband, in the presence of his wife, complained to a friend, "There was a time when my wife used to bring my shoes and my dog used to bark. Now things have reversed. My shoe is brought by my dog, and my wife barks." The wife had a good sense of humour and she immediately said to her husband, "Why are you complaining? You get both the things right. You get the shoe and also the bark!"

There was another husband. He was tall and hefty. The wife was short and slim. One day they entered into an argument. In the course of the argument the husband lost his temper and said to his wife, "If I liked, I could swallow you up." The wife had a sense of humour. She laughed as she said, "If you swallowed me up, you would have more brains in your belly than in your head!"

A husband said, "My wife has made me a millionaire." "What were you before you married her?" he was asked. And he answered: "A multimillionaire!"

It was a wise man who said that love can grow strong and healthy when it is nourished by a sense of humour. Unfortunately, married couples seem to be losing the ability to laugh with each other, or indeed laugh at themselves.

The world seems to have grown very serious nowadays. We tend to look at life solemnly. We have even begun to equate maturity with seriousness. We believe that wisdom cannot be accompanied by laughter.

More often than not, when people get together nowadays, be it at a party or club, the conversation often turns to morose issues – the crime rate, violence in society, rising taxes and prices, falling incomes or the polluted environment in which we live. I often wonder, "Where did all the fun and laughter go? What happened to the light-hearted banter people used to enjoy so much.?"

I would like to tell my married friends – it is a sad day, an incomplete day in your life, if you have not laughed together heartily at least thrice!

There is a little child in all of us who never ever grows old – no matter what our age. He needs to be coaxed to come out and play. True, life is a serious business and requires our deliberate consideration and thoughtful response. But a little fun and laughter now and then does plenty of good for everyone!

A young man and his bride-to-be were discussing their approaching marriage. "Now I want you to understand this clearly," he said firmly. "I'm going to be the boss in the house and you will do as I say."

He looked pleadingly at her as he continued, "Darling, please say yes!"

A young lady said to her fiancé, "Doctors say that married men live longer than bachelors."

"I've heard that too," nodded the young man gravely. "However, my married friends claim that it only *seems* longer!"

"How come you never married?" a man was asked.

"Oh well," he sighed. "It's like this you see – I kept looking for the ideal woman!"

"So you did not manage to find her then?"

"As a matter of fact I did! But it was my rotten luck – she was looking for the ideal man and she wouldn't have me!"

The little boys and girls in the Sunday school were earnestly preparing for their catechism – question - and-answer session – before their confirmation. Soon the Bishop himself arrived and the 'examination' began.

"What is matrimony?" the Rev. Father asked a nervous little girl.

"Ah...oh...mmm... it's a place where souls suffer for some time on account of their sins!" she blurted out.

"No, no Belinda," the parish priest chided her. "That's purgatory!"

"Who are we to correct her?" said the Bishop, tongue-in-cheek. "For all you know, she may be right! After all, what do you and I know about it?"

When the late Mr. and Mrs. Henry Ford celebrated their Golden Wedding Anniversary, a reporter asked them, "To what would you attribute the success of your married life?"

"The formula," said Ford, "is the same formula that I have always used in making cars – just stick to one model!"

It is said that the problems in marriage arise because a man often shows his worst side to his better half. I would say to such men – make your wife laugh, and you'll show her your best side!

It is also said that before marriage a man yearns for a woman. However, after the marriage the 'y' is silent. I would say to the wives – make your husbands laugh, and you will have deserved every penny he earns!

"Every woman should marry, and no man," said Disraeli. I would interpret that as a compliment to the women – for they are better equipped to handle a marriage with all its attendant stress and tension.

"Marriage halves our griefs, doubles our joys and quadruples our expenses," it is said. Don't you think that no expense can be too high for a woman who has devoted her entire life to you?

A French proverb tells us, "A good husband should be deaf and a good wife blind". I think that it is a little unkind. But it was a woman, Helen Rowland, who said, "To be happy with a man you must understand him a lot and love him a little. To be happy with a woman you must love her a lot and not try to understand her at all."

The brilliant comedian, Peter Ustinov, once said, "Marriage is like a three-speed gearbox: affection, friendship, love. It is *not* advisable to crash your gears and go right through to love straight away. You need to ease your way through. The basis of love is respect, and that can be learnt only through affection and friendship."

Humour is an all-round tonic: it promotes your physical, mental and emotional well-being. A woman once said to me, "My husband and I have been married for twelve months, but in all those times, he has smiled at me only three times!" Surely, that was a marriage which needed the all-round tonic of humour!

It is said that Adam asked God, "Oh God, why did you make Eve so beautiful?"

"So that you may love her," God replied.

"But then, why did you make her so stupid?"

"Otherwise she would never love *you*," he was told.

It was the 20th Wedding Anniversary of a couple and the wife found the husband sitting alone in his study – crying, shedding bitter tears.

"Don't be so sentimental," she said to him, giving a big hug. "Look at you! There are tears in your eyes!"

"I'm not being sentimental," sobbed her husband. "I was thinking of the day, 20 years ago, when your father caught us on the back-seat of my car, whispering sweet nothings into each other's ear. And he said to me, 'If you don't marry my daughter, I'll see that you go to jail for 20 years.'"

"But that's ok, silly," said the wife soothingly. "Here we are, safe and securely married!"

"I know," shuddered the husband. "If I had chosen the other option, I would have been a free man today!"

"Marriages are made in Heaven," says an anonymous statement, "but then so are thunder and lightning."

Don't lose the joy of living! Don't get trapped in daily chores, rituals, work and TV. Discover the zest of living. A happy family thrives on games, fun and laughter. Laughter and play, experts tell us, are therapeutic. Involve the children in your fun and games. Revel in their spontaneity and unselfconscious fun!

Laughter diffuses stress and tension. It promotes relationships and improves communication. It firms up the bonding between you and your spouse.

Pooja was a young wife and mother. She and her husband were to host a dinner party for his boss and colleagues, to celebrate his recent promotion. It was the first major party that she was hosting at home, and she was very nervous and tense. There was a load of work to be done too – straightening the house, cooking the dinner, setting out the crockery and cutlery, getting fresh flowers and so on and so on. How would she manage it all, Pooja wondered.

Seeing the mother's tension, the baby too became irritable and began whining and whimpering. After several attempts to comfort him and coax him failed, Pooja picked him up, kissed his forehead and tickled his tummy.

To her surprise and delight, the baby began to giggle and his laughter was infectious. He demanded more and more of the same treatment. Pooja would place a dish in the oven, wipe her hands, and go over to kiss and tickle the baby. He continued to giggle and laugh happily until she put the ice-cream to set in the freezer and came back to him. The sound of the baby's laughter gurgled like a flowing stream in the house, and before long, Pooja too, was smiling and singing as she attended to the pressing chores, one by one.

Need I say that the dinner was a grand success?

A little laughter can change the day. A child's happy giggle, a joke shared between the couple, or even the chuckle over a funny event in the past! When things get you down, do not explode in anger and stress. Find a reason to laugh — and you will see that anger and stress simply melt away! Truly, a good laugh can let sunshine and warmth into your home and your marriage!

Ninth Commandment Of Marriage : If Ever There Is A Misunderstanding, Do not Hide Your Feelings

Do not hesitate in discussing whatever is in your heart freely and without fear.

Many people have grown up in families where there was constant quarrelling and arguments. I dare say underneath all the noise and strife, these families really loved each other; but the trouble was that they only knew how to express anger – not how to express love. As a result, children of these families grew up thinking that expressing anger was also a way of expressing love. Yelling and shouting had become part of their psyche.

Equally, there are others who grew up thinking that anger was meant to be suppressed. It had never been expressed in their families.

There are safe and appropriate ways to express anger in a loving relationship. It has been said that anger is an opportunity to know yourself better.

Rakesh and Leela were peculiar in that they never ever expressed their anger. Rakesh would be seething with anger as Leela spoke to her friend on the telephone for hours together but he would not tell her so. He would decide to be generous and 'get over it' – but it rankled inside!

Leela was just the same. She hated the way he threw about his things here and there; shoes under the table, tie on the back of the chair, specs on the TV and so on. But she would never ever tell Rakesh that it upset her.

They both bottled up with their anger so effectively that the pressure was building up inside, and they were unaware of it. One fine day, there was a small mishap – Leela sank onto an armchair on which Rakesh had left his specs and the expensive glasses broke in two. And the most appalling fight ensued, in which they brought out all their stored-up resentments, grievances and complaints dating to their first meeting. "You did this…." "You were always like this…" "If only you knew…"

159

You remember my earlier suggestion to you – never to let the sun rise on your quarrel? Let me put the same idea across in a different way now: settle your accounts every night before you fall asleep. Clean up your relationship every night so that no 'issues' are pending and no grudges are carried forward. In fact, I would even encourage you to ask each other, "Is there anything you wish to tell me before we go to sleep?"

Your wife might say, "I took a lot of trouble to prepare a new dessert for dinner. I expected you to compliment me. Why didn't you?"

Or your husband might say, "Why did you scream at the servant this morning? You know how I hate it when you lose your temper."

You may have some explanations to offer, perhaps an apology to add and the issue is settled. Nothing is allowed to build up; nothing is carried forward. And tomorrow can start on a fresh, clean note.

It has rightly been said that the healthy flow of love and affection in a marriage is controlled by the nature and frequency of the communication between husband and wife. Communication that has been withheld or postponed or suppressed during the day can be conveyed at night, and all misunderstandings cleared up. This will enable you to go to sleep in a happy frame of mind.

When you communicate effectively and constructively, you can resolve issues much more satisfactorily.

Raju and Rita owned a large station-wagon. Raju loved to take weekend trips and long driving holidays with the children, and the hatchback car was ideal for his purpose. Rita was the one who did the shopping and attended to bills and banking and other chores. She found it difficult to manoeuvre and park the car on crowded streets and shopping centres. She wanted to go in for a smaller car and of course Raju would not hear of it. They argued, they fought about it bitterly.

"Get rid of this huge monster!" said Rita with gritted teeth.

"Do you think money grows on trees?" Raju retorted. "We are not changing the car now."

When you begin to argue like this, you end up going around in circles. You are unlikely to find a solution – a resolution – to the problem.

I urge couples to adopt the win-win attitude in such cases. Rita could tell her husband, "Darling, I find it very difficult to park the car nowadays. I am so scared I'll hit something or dent the car. What do you suggest I should do?"

Raju could be a little more sympathetic. "Should we hire a part-time driver so that the pressure is off you?" he could ask. Or, "Do you think we can budget for a smaller car – a second car for you?"

There is always a way in which both of you are winners!

Very often, it is the *men* who do not take the time and effort to share and communicate with their wives. A woman whose husband is uncommunicative begins to feel emotionally deprived. This may even lead to psychological disorders like depression, compulsive shopping or excessive eating. After all, no one likes to be taken for granted. Your wife is not a piece of furniture – nor is she your cook, housekeeper or the children's nanny! It is in *your* interest to actively share your life with her, and participate in her interests and concerns.

The truth perhaps is, that women look for much more from a marriage than men do. They need a deeper level of communication and companionship than men do. A merely physical relationship will not satisfy them. They require a sense of participation, involvement and understanding. These are achieved only through effective communication.

Marriage counsellors in the West say that they often come across couples, who, after 35 – 40 years of married life, claim that they cannot understand their partners. Perhaps this is becoming true of India also.

This is likely to happen when the spouses are self-centred, each focussing only on his/her interests and desires. I would like to tell such people: understanding your wife is more important than giving her a diamond necklace. Communicating lovingly with her is far more precious than sending her chocolates and flowers. When your wife begs you to spend an evening with her, you cannot put her off by saying: "Here is some money, go and do some shopping for yourself." What she needs is for you to share, participate in her life – not offer her an expense account!

It is vital in a happy marriage, for both partners to accept each other as *equals*. Marriage is a wonderful bond of companionship where no partner has to feel inferior or superior. If you do not treat your partner as an equal – beware, there is something wrong with your attitude! Love, understanding and mutual respect are the fundamentals of a happy marriage – and that exists only among equals.

Alas! It is so easy for us to analyse the other person and correct his/her faults, rather than to look to our own! We attempt to control others rather than change our attitudes!

If you wish to eliminate misunderstandings, if you wish to grow in the spirit of understanding and appreciation – talk, communicate effectively – but do not argue! Let your disagreements never become heated or violent. When you are emotionally overwrought you raise your voice, you condemn the other person, you lose your temper – and a bitter fight is bound to ensue.

After all, we are human, and disagreements and misunderstandings are bound to occur. But be quick to soothe and heal the wounds and rebuild your sense of understanding and commitment by keeping the communication channels open.

Is it so very difficult to say, "I'm so sorry, I shouldn't have said that? Is it so tough to say, "Forgive me, I won't let this happen again"?

It is alright to allow your partner to express his anger, if only you can remain calm and tolerant in the process. If each of you does it in turn, ego-clashes can be eliminated from your marriage. The truth is, arguments do not ever lead to amicable conclusions. Discussion, on the other hand will help you understand and appreciate the other's point of view.

As I have said repeatedly, God has made each of us unique. Diversity, difference is the spice of life – for if we all thought, spoke, acted and reacted alike, the world would be a dull and boring place. Life would become utterly predictable!

You don't have to agree on everything – but you don't have to argue all the time, either. It is far more civilised to talk things over; and it takes maturity and wisdom to appreciate the other person's point of view.

Let me also add – you must know yourself well, before you communicate effectively with your partner. It has been said, "Two people begin to fight when they do not understand each other's language." What is referred to here is not the language of voice and words – but the language of the heart, love. Know yourself. Assess your own strengths and weaknesses before you judge another person!

Avoid negative suggestions, hostile judgements – like "You are selfish," "You don't care," "You don't look good", etc.

Our children, particularly, suffer from such negative influences. "You are naughty," says the mother. "You are lazy and stupid," the father adds for his part. "This is a mistake," says the teacher. How unfortunate that none of them points to the child's good qualities and strengths!

Try to eliminate from your marriage all those negative tendencies which detract from love! Stop judging, stop accusing the other. Take joy in knowing your partner better. If you learn to understand, learn and accept your spouse, your children and your family members, your marriage will truly be transformed into a wonderful relationship.

The Question Of Equality

One of the most unfortunate 'developments' in the modern age is that the all-pervasive spirit of competition has even managed to enter the sacred sphere of marriage. I do not wish to say much about men's or women's liberation, but it is tragic if they are allowed to divide marriages.

Men and women were made to be different. God, in His wisdom, meant them to complement each other. I do *not* subscribe to the theory of women as "the weaker sex." They are not weaker – they are different, that's all! The husband's and wife's roles in marriage are *different* – and one cannot be played by other, no matter what young men and women think today. A woman is strong in qualities of the heart – sensibility and sympathy. The man is strong in qualities of the head. They should blend their selves together so that the union is wholesome and meaningful.

Women are strong in spiritual *shakti*. Biologically too, they can tolerate more pain. They are much better at handling stress. Fewer women die of heart-attacks. They endure suffering and adversity in ways that men cannot. That is why they have been described as "shock absorbers".

Yes, in many ways women are spiritually and emotionally stronger than men. This is why it is up to the woman to establish, strengthen and nurture the institution of marriage.

Both men and women go to work outside the home these days. Man is no longer the "sole breadwinner" as he was earlier. The wife is also a "provider" now.

But as a "provider" her responsibility is greater than his. Her role as a mother is crucial to the family and the future of the children. She, and *only* she can provide the secure, loving environment which is vital as the foundation for a child's life.

Fathers cannot shirk their responsibility. Their love and attention helps to expand the child's horizon as he grows older. " Workaholics" who neglect their duties to their children and families actually damage their own lives.

What we need today are men and women who are committed to the ideal of creating happy, healthy, harmonious families. Women should be allowed to grow and develop in every way – physically, emotionally, intellectually, and spiritually. But they should not imitate men or indeed compete with them!

Women have been exploited and discriminated against. This has led to a sense of insecurity and anger. We should learn to respect women – respect, revere and love them. But women, too, should accept their responsibility as creators of the home, as mothers, as guardians and custodians of the sacred institution of marriage. This requires that they attain inner harmony and serenity. Then will our homes be centres of peace, joy and love!

Marriage is for giving, not for taking. We cannot demand anything from our families – you are there to love them and serve them, and not the other way round. If you are a husband, I urge you to be devoted to your wife. If you are a wife, I entreat you to love and cherish your husband. You are both meant to be custodians and caretakers of the children!

Tenth and The Most Important Commandment of Marriage: Every Day You Must Find Time to Sit Together and Praise The Lord and Thank Him for having Brought the Two of You Together

You must spend some time together in the presence of God. It has been said, that the family that prays together, stays together. I have never come across a couple in serious difficulty who were praying together. If ever you have a disagreement or a problem, take it to God and, somehow, the solution will come. In God's presence we cannot argue with bitterness, in God's presence we cannot shout at each other. Let your life be rooted in the love of God and in the loving service of God's suffering children – and you will be richly blessed and be a source of blessing to many, on the rough road of life!

I urge all my friends: if you want to build a happy home and family, bring God back into your home. I am afraid many of us today have thrown God out of our homes. This has created a vacuum – and when there is a vacuum created in life, the devil rushes in to fill it!

Bring God back into your home so that the devil can have no place there. One way to do this is for the family to spend some time together daily, in God's presence. All the members of the family from the oldest to the youngest must get together for at least 15 minutes in God's presence, and hold a brief 'prayer meeting'. You can sing the Lord's Name, chant your favourite *mantra*, do a little *kirtan* or have a reading from the scriptures or the words of your guru. You can pick up a thought-for-the day from a great thinker and each of you can say what you feel about it.

Another way of asserting God's presence in your home is to put up a big, beautiful portrait of your *ishta devta*, or the picture of a great, holy soul who inspires you. Put it up in a very prominent position in the house, preferably so that you can see it from the entrance. Everytime any of you leave the home, you may bow in reverence before the picture, close your eyes and offer a brief prayer.

God is the source of all that is good in life. He is the source of understanding, tolerance, insight, patience, and love. It is easy to acquire these virtues when you put yourself in His hands.

When you pray together, you restore peace, balance and harmony to your marriage and family. When you take a disagreement or misunderstanding to God, you remove it from the realm of human bitterness.

There is a story of a man who dreamt that he went up to the divine storehouse where God kept all the marvellous gifts that He bestows on mankind. The man said to the angel in charge, "I'm sick and tired of all the miseries, ill-will and strife on earth, can you give me love, joy, peace and justice?"

The angel smiled and answered, "We don't stock fruits – only seeds."

Happy marriages are not handed over to anyone on a platter. You have to work hard at it – but God can give you all the help and inspiration that you need!

According to our ancient Hindu ideals, the husband worships *Devi* (goddess) Herself in his wife. So too, the wife worships God in her husband. Both worship God in the child. When you imbibe this ideal, you become conscious that God is within each one of us, and you love and serve God when you cherish the members of your family. As you can see, this is a way of elevating human relationships, and making marriage and family life a means of moving towards God. This is indeed the greatest spiritual goal of *grihasta ashrama*.

Let God be the focus of your home. Surrender yourselves to God, put your problems and difficulties before Him. Seek guidance from Him – not only in adversity, but at all times.

The Hindu epics and *puranas* offer us a glorious and inspiring vision of the ideal marriage. Who can fail to be inspired by the story of Ram and Sita? Who would not be moved by the story of Savitri and Satyavan? How many valuable lessons may we learn from the story of Nala and Damayanti? These blessed couples were indeed ideals, embodiments of perfection – but we can always emulate their example to the extent we can! Loyalty, selflessness, fidelity, constancy, understanding and patience are all wonderful qualities and these are the true ornaments of marital love.

One of the greatest responsibilities of a married couple is to bring forth good children. Your children not only carry forward your lineage and the name of your family – they must also be good human beings who contribute to the welfare of the world at large. *Vasudaiva Kutumbakam* is the Hindu ideal, which perceives the world as one family. Your children must be a blessing upon you and the world-family to which we all belong!

Set a good example for your children to emulate. Let them be brought up in an atmosphere of good words, right actions and high thinking.

An ancient story is told in the *puranas* about a pious mother who sang the following words in a cradle-song to her newborn infant:

Shuddhosi Buddhosi

Niranjanosi Samsara Maya

Parivarjitosi...

Translated, the inspiring words mean the following: "O child, you are not the body, you are the spirit; you are enlightened, you are the pure *atman* – the spirit. You are free of the taints of the world process."

I repeat – it is the greatest responsibility of a married couple to bring forth good children, to nourish them in love and care, to contribute in every manner possible to their spiritual, emotional, mental and physical well-being, and to promote their spiritual growth. I hope and pray that no married man or woman will ever neglect this sacred duty!

In marriage, you must seek to be the ideal, dedicated partner, a companion to your spouse in spiritual evolution. When a married couple lose sight of this high ideal, their marriage can be nothing more than a convenient arrangement. Any marriage that does not rise above motivations of physical desire, social advancement and financial considerations will become merely a bondage. How then, can the couple seek self-realisation or liberation from such bondage?

When the spiritual element enters marriage, when the presence of God is asserted in the marriage, then that marriage is truly made in heaven. It becomes the supreme highway on which two linked souls walk towards one ultimate goal. They are linked to each other through golden chains of love, understanding, devotion and piety. As we all know, when we have a loving travel-companion, the journey is easy and quick!

Let me stress, being attuned to God, being devoted to the spiritual goals does not mean neglecting your spouses and their needs and concerns! Rather I urge you to behold God in your spouses – offer love and respect and affection to them. Appreciate all that they are and all that they do. Fulfil your duties and responsibilities in the marriage and be an ideal companion to your partner.

When we hand our lives over to God in loving trust, He will do what is right for us. When we face a tough situation or a troublesome phase in family relationships, our first response should be to turn to God for help. Let Him be our friend, guardian, guide and counsellor! Let Him be fully involved in our lives!

"The family," said the Blessed Mother Teresa, " is the place to learn God. God created the family – together as husband, wife and children – to reflect His love."

Prayer opens up the flood gates of God's infinite mercy and power – allowing it all to flow into your

176

life. God does help and protect us even when we do not ask Him. But it is wonderful when we choose to invite Him into our lives. By so doing, we, too, participate in His work!

Leonard Raverhill says of prayer, "One might estimate the weight of the world, tell the size of the celestial city, count the stars of Heaven, measure the speed of lightning, and predict the time of the rising and setting sun – but you cannot even estimate prayer power! Prayer is as vast as God because He is behind it. Prayer is as mighty as God because He has committed Himself to answer it!"

Harness His power to your marriage and you will lack nothing!

Dada J.P. Vaswani's inspirational books have reached out to thousands of readers worldwide, communicating, as only he can, his practical, down-to-earth approach to life and living, helping people to overcome problems and challenges and make the most of the great gift that is human life!

Dada's philosophy is not theoretical – it is the art of daily living; his spirituality is not abstract – it consists simply of thinking good thoughts, speaking good words and doing good deeds; his God is love, his religion is service and sacrifice. Dada is the very embodiment of humility and love.

Dada ennobles and illumines everything he touches. His books have proved to be bestsellers, and have been translated into several languages in India and across the world.

Admired and revered as one of the outstanding spiritual leaders of modern India, Dada has reached out to the hearts and spirits of people wherever he has travelled. Dada's exciting, new books in the *Life Guides* Series, have been compiled from the inspiring, uplifting talks that he has delivered to enthralled audiences all over the world.